MW01124878

Famous Biographies for Young People

FAMOUS
PUERTO RICANS

by Clarke Newlon

ILLUSTRATED WITH PHOTOGRAPHS

Dodd, Mead & Company · New York

FRANKLIN SQ. PUBLIC LIBRARY
19 LINCOLN ROAD
FRANKLIN SQUARE, N.Y. 11010

The poems by Luis Palés Matos, "La Danza Negra" and "Danzarina Africana," are used with the permission of Editorial Universitaria, University of Puerto Rico, San Juan. The translation of "Danzarina Africana" is by Marlene Weiss. The poem by Cóncha Meléndez is the translation by Cynthia Maus which appears in her book, *Puerto Rico in Pictures and Poetry,* published by The Caxton Printers, Ltd., Caldwell, Idaho, and is used by permission of the publishers.

Copyright © 1975 by Clarke Newlon
All rights reserved
No part of this book may be reproduced in any form
without permission in writing from the publisher
Printed in the United States of America
by Vail-Ballou Press, Inc., Binghamton, N.Y.

Library of Congress Cataloging in Publication Data

Newlon, Clarke.
    Famous Puerto Ricans.

    Includes index.
    1. Puerto Rico—Biography—Juvenile literature.
I. Title.
CT526.N48   920'.07295   75-11436
ISBN 0-396-07149-X

ACKNOWLEDGMENTS

The staff members at both the Boricua Research and Resources Center and the Puerto Rican Commonwealth Library in Washington, D.C., were generous in helping me assemble the material for this book, in particular Julia Ann Howe and Marlene Weiss, Elba Martinez and Liza Fiol-Matta.

Professor Ernesto J. Ruiz de la Matta and Jorge Felices, both on the staff of Resident Commissioner Benítez, contributed incidents and details in the lives of two friends who are subjects of the book: artist Julio del Valle and poet Luis Palés Matos. Señora Beatriz de la Matta of the Commonwealth Bureau of Tourism was helpful with both information and photographs.

Paquita Vivo, who is resident of both San Juan and Washington and a working specialist on her native island, is superb as a consultant, advisor, and researcher.

Maurice Antonio Ferré, who contributed the Foreword, deserves special thanks. A word about his background follows his introductory remarks.

FOREWORD

In the English-speaking world, relatively little is known
of Puerto Rico. That is, perhaps, natural; the world is big,
Puerto Rico is small. The world today has a population of
close to 4 billion people of which less than 270 million—7
per cent—speak the Spanish language. Of this figure, approximately 4.5 million are Puerto Rican, or of Puerto
Rican descent, with approximately 1.5 million living in
the continental United States. That means that 4.5 million United States citizens are of Puerto Rican descent,
out of maybe 15 million Spanish-speaking residents of
the United States. It is an important minority of this
country. More should be known, not only about Puerto
Rico, but about Puerto Ricans.

In the United States there is now, and there has been
historically, a conflict between pluralism and consensus.
Pluralism is the multifaceted diversity of varying cultural
patterns of a society living together. Consensus is the difficult, but key, ingredient for establishing direction
through the will of the majority in a democratic society.
Consensus is never stable and is always in flux. Sometimes
our country takes directions against consensus. The consensus in America twenty years ago was for segregation—
this has now changed. The consensus fifteen years ago
was for U.S. involvement in Vietnam—that, too, changed.
Government action does not always follow consensus—yet

it remains an essential, although at times elusive, primary ingredient in our form of government. The conflict between pluralism and consensus in the United States is due to the fact that the majority of the nation, Anglo-Saxon in its heritage or assimilation, wants the remaining minorities to blend into the oneness which they believe is essential for Americanism. A large number of the minorities, on the other hand, keep their individual culture, which they see as the basis for pluralism in the United States. So the key question arises. Must all minorities melt into the generalness of Americanism, or can they maintain cultural distinction, and yet be good American citizens? In the past the answer to "Must you melt into the pot?" has been an ambiguous "Yes." Swedes and Italians alike had to melt into the mainstream of American life by losing their previous cultural identity and becoming Anglo-Saxonized, not only in language, but also in spirit.

Blacks, although born in the United States, could not in fact be totally free, that is, free to participate, because they could not conform and become Anglo-Saxonized, due to skin color. On the other hand, they could not go back to Africa, nor was Africa meaningful to them, except as history. It was only when blacks forced the issue upon the majority—that is, those who formed the consensus of the majority—that they too, not only under the law but in effect, had a place in the sun of this country. The Black minority has now, under the "new" guideline, begun to attain equality as American citizens. The simple phrase, "Black Is Beautiful," captures in three words volumes of books. That simple but important and, in our case, revolutionary concept has permeated throughout the last twenty years of the American experience. The incident at Selma flowed into Wounded Knee and into the grape fields of the Napa Valley in California.

American sociologists have now followed the pattern of this past quarter century, where the exertions of these minorities have been made in joining the mainstream, that is, the American dream, but not following the same pattern as before. And so we now read books about the unmeltable minorities. The dynamism of this process does not go unchallenged. There are many who feel alienation from and to the process, and insist on the historic assimilation of these minorities. Their insistence is ironic, because it is these very same people who, with their "Archie Bunker mentality," have kept back to now the assimilation of these minorities into the mainstream of American society. The worst indictment of this collective restriction was our treatment of the American Indian. Worse than Black slavery because, in addition to the removal of their personal freedom by being placed on reservations, we took their land. Subjugated by brute force, these original Americans were requested to "Americanize," that is, to negate their culture and assume that of the new majority. Despite the oppression of squalor and alcohol, to this date total "Americanization" has not happened to our Indians. They have maintained their cultural identity—their nationality—although they have accepted with pride United States citizenship.

Meanwhile, in Puerto Rico the problems of identity continue. The question of "Who am I as a Puerto Rican?" is clear to only a few. The majority are confused between their loyalty between the big *"patria"* and the little *"patria."* This is nothing new; the problem was the same when the Spanish flag flew over Puerto Rico. The modern, confused Puerto Rican wrongly assumes that a man cannot have more than one loyalty. It is like saying there is a conflict between the moral order and the civil order. In other words, like saying that religious entities cannot involve themselves in civic matters, or that the government cannot involve itself in moral questions. Or—can a Jew feel loyal to his religion, to his culture, to Israel, and to the United States all at the same time? Can a Catholic president distinguish between his oath of loyalty to uphold the Constitution, and at the same time follow the mandates of the Holy Father in Rome who, if you are Catholic, is believed to be infallible in matters of doctrine? These are gray areas, areas of possible conflict. Nevertheless, or despite these nebulous areas, most honest men of good will have found a balanced sense of loyalty that, by being multifaceted, one aspect of the whole strengthens the other.

From Aristotle to Jacques Maritain, there has been a clear but concise distinction between nation and state, between citizenship and nationality. This distinction is clear, and yet, because of our emotions, we so often refused to see what is logically "simple." There is no reason why a Puerto Rican cannot maintain loyalty to several concepts, not exclusive of each other. I can be an American citizen, completely loyal to my flag and country, but that does not preclude my being a proud Puerto Rican, or even in a broader sense, of identifying and maintaining loyalty to my Hispanic culture. As Rubén Darío and Salvador Madariaga both stated, we who speak the Spanish language on this side of the Atlantic are but an extension of "Spain." That does not mean that we are all citizens of the same country, nor that we believe in the same political process, or even that we do not have our own particular cultural distinctions. But rather, it means that we can find a common base in the same way that an Argentine, different as he may be from a Colombian, can still identify with a Mexican; no different than an Englishman having empathy and a common bond with an Australian or a Canadian—different in some things, similar in many.

For years there have been those who recognize the important role Puerto Rico and Puerto Ricans can play as a bridge between the great cultures of the north and south of the hemisphere. It is a valid role.

The identity problem in Puerto Rico is complicated—in some cases, because people cannot make a distinction between citizenship and nationality, and in others, because they consciously make a distinction, that is, in their minds they can equate nationality and citizenship into one. The latter strongly feel that to be Puerto Rican means one nationality, one citizenship; they are mainly for the independence of Puerto Rico as a political solution to status. Others, who can distinguish the inherent difference, are for statehood as a final solution to political status. The remainder—in this case, the majority—are those who want a Commonwealth form of government as a final status.

Most Puerto Ricans on the island, who almost in their totality have had some sort of schooling, do not need this book, as they are well aware of who Roberto Clemente was and who Luis Muñoz Marín is. This book serves mostly the general English-speaking American public and those Puerto Ricans who live on the mainland and may not be totally aware of "their people."

It is not a complete biography. The title is, in a sense, a

misnomer. It is not a biography of famous Puerto Ricans, but rather thumbnail sketches of some famous Puerto Ricans. The absence of many, like Hostos, De Diego, Jose Ferrer, to name but a few, is lamentable, but there must be a limit. Although I would have chosen different Puerto Ricans, I certainly would not have omitted any of the ones Mr. Newlon has selected.

In some cases, Mr. Newlon's style is journalistic and some of the biographies read like news for the morning paper; others are more traditionally biographical. This is a matter of style; it lends ease of reading to the subject at hand.

In varying degrees in these thumbnail sketches, we find out not only why, but how and who these people are. I am sure the intent of the author is that the reader follow up and, perhaps through further reading, find out more of the particular famous Puerto Ricans of interest.

There is much social connotation and implication in these biographies, but that, of course, is a reflection of the times and of the people themselves. The author weaves the threads of adversity and of hardship, racial and sex discrimination into a pattern which clearly indicates that Puerto Ricans, like other minorities, have had to fight for their successes and have also overcome and achieved.

Antonio Paoli, the great Puerto Rican tenor, is not himself sketched in this series, but he is mentioned in the biography of Justino Díaz. Carmen Maymi is followed by Roberto Clemente, also black, who is then followed by Páles Matos, the great "Black Poet of the Antilles," and the great interpreter in the Spanish-speaking world of the African psyche. One naturally assumes that Páles

Matos was also black, but he was fair-skinned, blue-eyed, and blond. This detail is not important, because that is precisely one of the beauties of the Puerto Rican people that also flows from this mixture of famous Puerto Ricans.

Clarke Newlon has been a newspaper reporter and editor, has many books to his credit, has lived in various parts of this country and in Europe and the Mediterranean. He is a man of obvious diversity, prepared to look into a different culture and, with a universal view, bring an objective look into biographies of some famous Puerto Ricans. It is an important step forward that should give hundreds of thousands, and hopefully millions, directly and indirectly, a better understanding as to who, and what, Puerto Ricans are.

What is important in the long run is not the individual success story of each Puerto Rican in this book, but rather the sun and shadow that their success casts among the rest of us of that culture. For those of us Puerto Ricans on the mainland it means a better understanding of ourselves, and for our non-Puerto Rican brethren, an insight not only into what we are but, more importantly, an insight into what we can become.

MAURICE A. FERRÉ
Mayor of Miami, Florida

Maurice Ferré is a remarkable Puerto Rican on several counts. In 1973, at the age of thirty-eight, he defeated six opponents to become Mayor of Miami, a city which has an enormous resident population of Hispanic origin, though Cuban of course and not Puerto Rican. Before that he had been chosen Man of the Year (by the Miami Jaycees in 1968), Florida's Democrat of the Year (1968), and Outstanding Young Man of Miami (1970).

In nonpolitical life he is president of Maule Industries, Inc., a company with numerous affiliates in the United States and rather widely proliferated throughout the Caribbean area. He was born in Puerto Rico where the Ferré family is sometimes equated dynastically with the Rockefellers on the mainland. The family home is in Ponce where Maurice's grandfather, Antonio Ferré, started a foundry in 1917. José Ferré, Maurice's father, laid the foundation for the family fortune in 1941–42 when he started a cement plant in Ponce which, with the advent of World War II, prospered rapidly and expanded widely, in Cuba, Venezuela, and later the United States. Luis Ferré, Maurice's uncle, was elected Governor of Puerto Rico in 1968 for a four-year term. He ran again unsuccessfully in 1972.

Maurice Ferré attended Laurenceville School in New Jersey and the University of Miami where he received a B.S. degree in architectural engineering. He also did graduate work in economics and finance. In 1955 he married Mercedes Malaussena of Venezuela and they have six children. He served in the Florida State Legislature in 1967 and on the Miami City Commission from 1967 to 1970. Since Miami has a city manager form of government, Maurice Ferré is able to carry a full work load as president of Maule Industries and also carry out the civic and political responsibilities of city leadership.

CONTENTS

Illustrations follow page 92

CONTENTS

16

PUERTO RICO

THE ISLAND OF Puerto Rico was discovered by Christopher Columbus on his second voyage of exploration and it was captured, more or less, by the United States four hundred years later as a prize of the Spanish-American War.

It is one of the West Indies. It is the southernmost island of the Greater Antilles. It has towering mountains and white sand beaches laved by the blue-green waters of the Caribbean, the most benevolent of climates, and a most romantic history.

Columbus landed on the island on November 19, 1493, led there from Guadeloupe, his first landfall, according to one legend, by a cluster of Arawak Indian women who had escaped the clutches of their Carib Indian captors and wanted to go home. Columbus, following his custom of reaching into the Bible for names, called the island San Juan Bautista for John the Baptist. Later, Ponce de León, struck by the beauty of the harbor when he sailed into it, exclaimed, "*Que puerto rico,*" but somehow the names got switched in cartographic copying; the island became Puerto Rico and the capital and principal city became San Juan.

The Indians, who were there first after all, called the island Boriquén and the word still clings, though the spelling is slightly altered. "Borinquen" is a popular trade

17

name throughout Puerto Rico and the national anthem is "La Borinqueña."

The Spanish, who built and based their vast empire in the New World upon the discoveries of Columbus, and the conquistadors who followed him, called the long line of what is now the Caribbean side of the Latin American coast *Tierra Firme,* and the English translated this term into Spanish Main. Drake, Hawkins, and other marauding privateers, mostly English, made the coastline and islands that Columbus had named the West Indies their happy hunting ground, and its winds, tides, and harbors became as familiar to them as those of the English Channel. Avoiding the fortress guns of the big harbors, they lurked in the thousand-and-one hiding places available, refurbishing their supplies as they waited, and then pounced on the Spanish galleons and merchantmen.

Gradually the Spanish Main as a geographical term became the entire Caribbean area (although that name itself had not yet been applied), extending from the island of Trinidad on the southeast clear to the North American Gulf Coast and Florida, and encompassing the literally thousands of islands from the Bahamas through the Barbados.

The westerly trade winds blow out of the Atlantic, cooling the subtropical climates of the Main. The Spanish found it pleasant four centuries ago and millions of travelers, traders, and tourists have found it the same since.

Only sparsely endowed with gold, silver, or precious gems—which is what the Spanish and all their competitors of the day wanted—but strategically located and happily endowed with its great harbor, Puerto Rico became important as a bastion of support for the Spanish Main.

Its fortresses of El Morro and San Cristóbal became the Gibraltar of the Caribbean, and San Juan harbor a safe haven for the vessels headed homeward silver-laden from Mexico and Peru. Sir Francis Drake tried to shoot his way past the harbor's guns in 1595 and had to turn tail and run, one of his few confusions at the hands of the Spanish. The Earl of Cumberland did find a weakness not long thereafter, landing some miles up from the fortifications and enveloping them from the land side. He occupied the city for less than six months and was driven out by an enemy more deadly than the Spanish—dysentery. The Dutch tried later and so did the English, again—both failing, though other islands of the Indies were changing hands with embarrassing frequency. The whole area of the West Indies was, of course, by both term and actuality, the cockpit of the New World, called so with a thought to the pit in which fighting cocks were loosed to kill one another.

Several of the battles in San Juan harbor had been narrow squeaks for the Spanish, to the point that it became apparent the city and island could eventually fall to one European power or another. To prevent this, construction of a great wall completely around the city was begun in 1631. Sections of it rose sixty feet above the harbor and it proved impregnable, though its most important strong point, Fort San Cristóbal, was not fully completed until 1778.

The first residents of Puerto Rico, as far as history knows, were the Arawak (sometimes known as Taino because "*taino*" was the word they called out in greeting) and the Carib Indians. Both were brown-skinned but the resemblance ended there. The Arawaks were gentle and peaceable. They had an elaborate social structure which arranged itself in layers from the headman on down, but the structure was hereditary and apparently functioned only casually, for the Arawaks had made peace with their environment and in so doing had discovered how to live pleasantly with the expenditure of a minimum amount of industry. They had originated on the mainland and occupied the islands of the Greater Antilles.

The Caribs, who also came from the Tierra Firme, were truculent, fiercely predatory and, by most accounts, cannibalistic. They had moved from the lower part of the subcontinent over to the southernmost island of the Lesser Antilles and were gradually working their way north and westward, island-hopping, so to speak. They apparently had just arrived on Puerto Rico and were prepared to take over from the Arawaks—who knew them of old—when Columbus arrived and beat them to it.

The Great Navigator, and the Spanish governors who followed him, discovered that the tractability of the Arawaks and their subjugation were two entirely different things. The Arawaks were happy to submit, particularly after their leaders had been put to the sword or the blazing pit, but submission did not include working. When the Spanish tried to make them slaves, the Arawaks simply preferred the alternative of death and accepted it, much to the frustration of their masters.

The Caribs, their spears no match for the Spanish muskets, took to the hills. From there they conducted an intermittent guerrilla operation which mostly consisted of slaughtering any Spaniard who was foolish enough to get too far from home by himself.

Eventually, however, they were wiped out also. It is

possible only to guess at the number of Indians, Arawaks, and Caribs on the islands when Columbus reached them, but the figure must have been in the millions. Today the Arawaks have disappeared completely, a lost tribe. There is a bare trace of the Caribs, a reservation on the western coast of Dominica. They live in conventional houses and play the English game of cricket and prefer to settle all of the arguments peaceably, completely and sadly domesticated.

Puerto Rico, when the Spanish arrived and presumably always, was virtually devoid of four-footed animal life except for rodents and the iguana and other smaller lizard types. The vast abundance of bird life, however, was remarkable. Columbus had arrived at the island just in time to witness the great fall migration which included clouds of ducks and geese, which both the Indians and the Spanish hunted for food, and scores of varieties of warblers and other songbirds. There were the tropical feathered residents, too, of course, and the Spanish seaman found the brilliantly plumed parrots easily caught, easily tamed, and easily taught to speak. And thus was furthered a tradition—the sailor and his parrot.

The Spanish introduced pigs to the island. They, later and on various occasions, escaped custody and became wild, furnishing pork roasts for generations of hunters to come. The Europeans also brought horses, of course. The first were the rough plough animals but later they introduced the Andalusians from which have evolved today's Puerto Rican breed, famous for its *paso fino,* a high-performance broken pace known as the "island gait."

No matter where they voyaged and conquered, or how far from Seville and in what climate, the Spanish took their customs with them. When they built a settlement, it was in the image of the Old World pattern. It had a great plaza or square with a church on one side and a large public building on another. And no matter that the sun was fiercely hot and the air humid and steamy, portraits and paintings of the period show them dressed in wool and silk and velvet, the men wearing a sword and frequently armor.

Columbus, who could navigate his crews halfway around the world through uncharted seas, couldn't steer them much of anywhere once they faced the problems of living on dry land. When this shortcoming became apparent in the great man, Spain's Queen Isabella replaced him as governor of the settlement he had founded on nearby Hispaniola (now Haiti and the Dominican Republic) with the practical and competent Nicolás de Ovando, who moved in a crew of farmers and artisans. And Ovando brought with him to the island a number of new crop plants. Among those which flourished were oranges and lemons, bananas, figs, rice, and sugar cane. These eventually were also shared by Puerto Rico. Sugar cane, of course, became an important harvest; distilled into rum, it was a major product of the island.

In a world and a time when wealth was measured in shiploads of bullion, Spain never regarded Puerto Rico as anything but a useful and at times necessary nuisance. Ponce de León, who had accompanied Columbus on his second voyage, was the first governor, and the home which was built for him is believed to be the oldest continually inhabited dwelling in the Western Hemisphere.

Through the centuries, the island had its ups and downs, mostly the latter. In the early 1530s it was visited by first an epidemic of the smallpox and then by a plague of ants, and was virtually abandoned for a time. It was neglected by Spain until its necessity as a safe haven on the route of the Spanish Main forced the mother country to make a levy against Mexico of half a million pesos a year for its support. The levy continued until Mexico rebelled against that and other things in the early nineteenth century. In 1600, Puerto Rico became a penal island.

Through the Treaty of Utrecht in 1713, which followed the eleven-year European war to prevent France from completely dominating Spain, several of the islands of the West Indies changed hands and Spain found herself with only Cuba and Puerto Rico left. They were really all she wanted, for, with the wealth of Mexico and South America piling up on her doorstep, the Spanish rulers had little taste for the small-time plantings of small-time islands. There was another reshuffling in 1815 with the signing of the Treaty of Vienna.

By this time Spain's colonies in the New World were melting away, not with a bang, except in the case of Mexico, but with a failure of the colony system. The mechanism of remote rule would no longer work automatically and Spain had not the power to do it by force. Spain might at that time have lost both Cuba and Puerto Rico to the evil intentions of the British had not President James Monroe announced that the United States would not tolerate any interference by foreign powers on the American continent, North or South, and this was clearly intended to include the islands of what had been the Spanish Main. In 1836, María Cristina, the Spanish Queen regent, almost sold Puerto Rico, along with Cuba and the Philippines, to France. It would have been a gross infringement of the Monroe Doctrine, but the deal fell through.

The nineteenth century, however, brought significant changes to the island. It also saw the population double to a million people. The changes were largely political and probably significant only to a small, educated, and well-to-do class of intellectuals who were sharing the ferment which was sweeping Spain's other American colonies. With what became an almost absurd inconsistency of rule, Spain gave and then took away civil and political liberties for the Puerto Ricans like a conjurer's sleight-of-hand tricks. The Constitution of 1812, reflecting the political reforms in Spain itself, was duly transmitted to Puerto Rico and other colonies. It permitted colonial representatives to the Spanish Cortes (Congress) and allowed other sovereign liberties. It was a great and a significant advance. But in 1814, two years later, the Constitution was abolished by King Ferdinand VII. It was restored in 1820 by the Riego Revolt, abolished again by Ferdinand in 1823, partly restored by María Cristina in 1834, and more fully by Queen Isabella II two years later.

In 1855, a terrible epidemic of cholera swept Puerto Rico, leaving a death count of thirty thousand persons and paralyzing the island for the next several years. In 1868 a small but enthusiastic revolt inland with the glamorous call of "Death or Liberty" became known in island history as the *Grito de Lares*, reminiscent of Father Hidalgo's famous *Grito de Dolores* in Mexico. Unfortunately, the revolt was so tiny that word of it didn't spread more than a few miles. San Juan didn't learn of it until long after it had settled into just a happening.

24

Reflecting still further reforms in the mother country, Puerto Rico was accorded the status of a province in 1870 and formed political parties for the first time. A trade agreement between Spain and the United States permitted the entrance of North American products into Spanish ports, including San Juan, at less than the heretofore ruinous tariffs, while Washington abolished its tax of 10 per cent on products from Puerto Rico and Cuba. A little later another agreement permitted the entrance of sugar from the two islands into the United States free of duty.

By 1897, the Puerto Rican political body had produced two major parties, one of which, under the leadership of young Luis Muñoz Rivera, founder and editor of the newspaper, *La Democracia,* had worked out a pact with the new liberal Spanish Prime Minister to obtain an autonomous charter for Puerto Rico. It gave the island virtually dominion status with representation at the Cortes, a bicameral legislature of its own, and many other powers of self-regulation. True independence seemed at hand—or almost—and Puerto Ricans, at least those who understood the importance of the Spanish concessions, were wild with joy.

It was into this atmosphere a few weeks later that the conquering North American army marched on July 25, 1898.

Due to the island's singular history, the people of Puerto Rico differed considerably from those of Cuba or those of the other islands of the Caribbean. The island had always been valued by Spain for its military worth, not because it might be productive of wealth. And because of this, the percentage of black slaves was never as great as in the other islands. The white race was always predominant. There had been, of course, a mingling of blood: Spanish with Indian, Spanish with Negro, Negro with Indian. And the offspring of these unions were *criollos,* a brown-skinned, finely featured people. The women were often marvelously beautiful, renowned for their charm and languid grace.

This same lack of productive wealth which resulted in Spain's frequent neglect also was the cause of Spain's lack of real pressure on the *puertorriqueños.* After the first greedy savagery of the conquistadors there were no gold quotas to fill, nor silver; actually, none of any kind. The island was largely left to subsist or go hungry, as it frequently did, but it never rose from apathy long or strong enough to actually rebel, as did Cuba. To only a few of the intellectuals did it ever occur to break away from Spain with whom they shared the heritage of language, customs, and religions. When Gerardo Forrest, a member of a revolutionary group in New York, visited Puerto Rico to discuss plans for a rebellion, one of the island's political leaders wrote him: "In all the country it would be difficult to find ten men who have sufficient valor to sacrifice themselves for the idea that you propose." And Luis Muñoz Rivera, the most influential politician of his era, told Forrest: "I am a partisan of independence as an ideal. . . . Nevertheless, I consider that the independence of my country is absolutely impossible . . . our masses never fought and will not. . . ."

Even less did it occur to them to link with the United States, with whom they had almost nothing in common, although most of the Puerto Rican leaders were uneasily aware of the "Manifest Destiny" philosophy which had been sweeping their big northern neighbor. This Manifest Destiny had already brought the United States the lands of Louisiana and Florida by purchase and a large hunk of Mexico by conquest.

But link they did, beginning that July morning when an American army led by General Nelson A. Miles landed at Guánica on the southeastern coast. The somewhat stunned Puerto Ricans welcomed the invaders, at least at first, and on July 28, 1898, General Miles issued a proclamation which read, in part:

"As a consequence of the war which necessitated action by the United States against Spain, in defense of Liberty, Justice, and Humanity, her military forces have come to occupy the Island of Puerto Rico . . . They bring you the armed support of a free nation, whose great power rests in her justice and humanity for all who live under her protection . . . The primary effect of this occupation will be the immediate transition from your former system of government, desiring that you accept joyfully the system of the Government of the United States."

After a period of two years and four military governors, none of whom were really accepted joyfully, the United States in 1900 passed the Foraker Act, an example of colonialism at its worst. It gave Puerto Rico a thirty-five-member House of Delegates elected by popular vote, but any legislation passed had to be approved by three different United States authorities. The Act did, however, permit the local election of a representative to the U.S. Congress who was entitled to speak on the floor but not to vote.

Muñoz Rivera was elected to that position and promptly became a gadfly who never permitted the members of Congress to forget that their political treatment of Puerto Rico had set back the island's sovereign rights a century or so. Muñoz Rivera's eloquence resulted in the passage, in 1917, of the Jones Act. This gave Puerto Rico a two-chamber legislature and greatly increased power. More important, the Jones Act also granted citizenship. Thirty years later, in 1947, the Congress gave the islanders the right to elect their own governor. The first man to fill that position was Luis Muñoz Rivera's son, Luis Muñoz Marín, who had been born just three days after the battleship *Maine* blew up in the harbor of Havana, triggering the Spanish-American War. And on July 25, 1952, fifty-four years (to the day) after the American invasion of the island, it was granted Commonwealth status. Thus ended, to a large degree, four and a half centuries of colonialism for Puerto Rico.

Uncle Sam was always a benign colonial master with the very best of intentions. The educational facilities on the island were increased a hundredfold. Children were inoculated against disease, the death rate dropped, the birth rate ascended. Roads were built. Mainland corporations bought up extensive land holdings for the cultivation of sugar and tobacco. In thirty years bank deposits grew from less than $2 million to some $54 million. A few people, some on the island but most of them on the mainland, reaped great profits.

Little if any of the money, however, filtered down to the poor. The younger Muñoz wrote that his island had become a land of millionaires and peons. And it was largely the latter.

In 1941, President Franklin D. Roosevelt sent one of his better aides, Rexford Guy Tugwell, to be governor. He, with a young Puerto Rican named Teodoro Moscoso, started the island on the road to an industrial program. Eight years later, when Tugwell had left and Muñoz Marín became the first elected governor, Operation Bootstrap was launched. It was a project to interest United States industrialists in investing in the island.

Bootstrap succeeded beyond the wildest of dreams. Hundreds of new manufacturing plants were established. Tourism became a flourishing industry. Big oil moved in and built millions of dollars' worth of refineries to handle millions of barrels of crude oil from Venezuela. Employment increased by the hundredfold. Thousands of barefoot *jíbaros* came down from the mountains and the hinterlands. Wages went up. So did neon signs, high-rises, and the birth rate.

In fact, Bootstrap succeeded so well that by the mid-1950s the island leaders launched Operation Serenity in an effort to slow it down, and to slow down also the "Americanization" of Puerto Rico, and to recapture something of the Spanish heritage, culture, and ambiance. But Bootstrap has proved to be a juggernaut; more developments, more concrete, more prosperity of a sort.

And today the people of this still lovely island are balanced between two philosophies of life—the old, the new. Or maybe even a third, something in between. The latter is actually more likely. It is doubtful the Puerto Ricans will ever really turn back the clock. Nor will they submit completely to assimilation.

CARMEN MAYMI
Activist

CARMEN ROSA MAYMI, director of the Women's Bureau of the United States Department of Labor, sees her job in one pragmatic dimension: to be the chief advocate of more than thirty-three million women workers.

When Carmen Maymi was a junior at De Paul University in Illinois, she was interviewed by the Chancellor on her application for scholarship assistance from the school.

"My father and mother had brought me to Chicago from Puerto Rico when I was fifteen," she relates, "so that I could be educated on the mainland and go to college. Father had been an accountant and city auditor at home. In Chicago he took the only job he could get, operating a foot-press machine at the minimum wage—$1.25 an hour. But he and my mother would never let me ask for help. My father had managed, and it must have been terribly hard, to pay for my tuition and expenses.

"But now, I had applied for a scholarship. My grades were among the highest in my class. My conduct and that sort of thing were okay and I certainly needed the money. Heaven knows we were poor enough.

"So that day I went in for the interview with the Chancellor. I can still remember every bit of it. He looked at me and then at my records and then back at me. And said: 'I'm not going to give you a scholarship. You're too pretty. Some boy will fall in love with you and you'll get married within two years after you graduate and the money will just have been wasted.' "

Carmen paused and looked out the window of her office at Fourteenth and Constitution Avenue, and then let her eyes roam around the big room with its wide desk and leather chairs, the divan and a conference table which seats twelve or more. It may have been a conscious gesture to herself, a way of telling herself how far she had come from the poverty of the Near Northwest side of Chicago.

"Then," she said, "I thought his reaction was racist— because I was a Puerto Rican and a black. Now I know it was because I was a woman. It was purely and blatantly sexist."

That, the sex factor which all working women encounter at some point and usually repeatedly throughout their working lives, is necessarily a preoccupation with Carmen. In a way it is her job.

"I have learned," she says, "that the common denominator of discrimination against women is sex, not race or even color, though they certainly come into it.

"Society has not faced up realistically to the fact that women are enlarging their role in the economic life of the nation and that they have come to a point where they realize their potential and demand equal rights and responsibilities in commerce and industry, in politics and government, and in social and cultural development."

And she will point out the statistics to prove her words. Today more than 44 per cent of all women sixteen years and older are in the work force. That is a gain of 11 per cent from 1960, when it was 33 per cent. The Labor Department estimates that by 1985 the figure will have climbed even higher and will be pushing the 50 per cent mark. And "Maybe by that time the movement for equal rights will be strong enough to accomplish some of the things we've been working toward."

Carmen Maymi was born on March 17, 1938, in Santurce, Puerto Rico, and it is quite possible the fact that it was St. Patrick's Day may not have occurred to her parents, Luis Maymi Garcia and Socoro Sierra Maymi. When she was three years old her father moved his little family to Toa Alta where he became city auditor and also practiced his profession of accountant. They lived in Toa Alta for five years and Carmen still has her first-grade school certificate, framed by her father.

The Toa Alta years were a happy time for the girl, an only child then and thereafter. The Maymis had a house on top of a minor mountain with a river winding its way around the base. Carmen had a pet pig, a gift from her father.

"I named the pig Tatita. The other kids had puppies and kittens and chickens. I had Tatita. She was very bright and I trained her to do a lot of small tricks but mostly she just followed me around."

Living in Toa Alta was much like living in the country and all three of the Maymis loved it. There were relatives nearby and there were many family gatherings. Carmen had a number of cousins, all of them boys but one.

"We were all musical. My father played the trumpet and we used to sing together a lot." Among their favorite songs were "Perfidia" and "El Jibarito." And they sang many of the dance melodies of the time. "We used to sing the *danzas* and dance to them, too," said Carmen. "My voice? It's alto and pretty good. Yes, I used to love to dance. I still do."

After five years in Toa Alta, Luis Maymi took his family back to Santurce, a suburb of San Juan. There he had a greater field for his profession and there Señora Maymi taught in the Castelar Elementary School, which Carmen attended.

School continued for Carmen in Santurce, through her mother's fourth-grade classroom and on into junior high. Carmen sang over the radio and probably could have had some sort of a career as a professional singer, but this was not in the future her parents envisioned for her.

"There was never any doubt that I would go to college," said Carmen. "It was simply assumed as a fact. There was lots of time for play. I loved the beach. We all did and we went practically every day. My family and all the cousins and aunts and uncles. We were certainly far from rich but we had enough money to lead a pleasant life.

"But I studied, I studied hard; I always did that, and I read everything in sight, good and bad. I can't understand people who want to restrict the reading of children. Give them everything. They'll learn to get selective.

"Whatever happened to Tatita when we left Toa Alta? Well, Tatita had a pretty good life. At least we probably thought it was. When Tatita got too big to be a comfortable pet we gave her to a cousin and Tatita started setting records having big families—ten and twelve babies at a time. The last time I heard, that is what she was still doing, though I suppose old age must have caught up with her by this time."

33

Carmen's father believed that an only child must be independent and able to stand on her own two feet.

"We always had an old jalopy of some kind around, usually a pickup truck. I could change a tire alone by the time I was eleven. And mother taught me to sew and embroider. There was also a big garden at Santurce with trees to climb. I had chickens there, and cats. Mother used to make me dolls out of cornhusks. I designed clothes for them. I used to build doll houses, too, and the chickens and the cats always wanted to come in."

When Carmen was fifteen, Luis Maymi brought this *buena vista* to an abrupt end by moving his family to Chicago. The shock of exchanging the gracious Hispanic culture and customs of Puerto Rico for the raw, racial-mixing mélange of Chicago, not to mention trading the friendliest climate on earth for the arctic winds which knife in off Lake Michigan, must have been traumatic.

"Yes," remembers Carmen, "it was a change, but it was exciting, too."

Luis Maymi established his little family on the Near Northwest side of Chicago, in a community largely made up of Polish, Italian, and Spanish-speaking residents. Incomes ranged from low to nonexistent. Carmen was enrolled in Wells High School which had about seven hundred pupils whose backgrounds reflected the neighborhood. Carmen's mother spoke English with difficulty, her father practically not at all, and Carmen herself could read English but had great trouble speaking it.

"The first year or so was very hard, and, of course, much of that was due to communication—or the lack of it. I was shy; or maybe I just hated to make mistakes. (I still do.) But during those first months, if I tried to talk and made a mistake early in the day—that was the end. I wouldn't open my mouth again. Some of the teachers were kind and understanding. Some were not. The principal had taught in Puerto Rico and that helped.

"We had gangs in the school and all of the rough business going on that you read of in the papers: gang wars, rumbles, that kind of thing. There were actually three factions: the blacks, the Spanish-speaking, and the parent-teacher group. I found myself sometimes in what seemed like the vortex of a whirlpool. I was a black, so the black gang claimed me. I was Spanish-speaking—and they claimed me. But I was also one of the best students in school, so the teachers wanted me on their side.

"I frequently found myself being the mediator," Carmen continued.

It was probably good training, at an early age, for her work in government. Here, she finds herself having to maneuver between often conflicting points of view, that of blacks, the Spanish-speaking, the women, and, not at all least, her employer, the federal government.

Others may have had trouble with Carmen's identity. She, herself, has none. "I have a pretty healthy concept of myself as a Puerto Rican, and a black. And being a woman comes quite naturally. But none of those says it entirely. I am myself. I am Carmen Maymi. That says it all."

From the age of fifteen when she arrived, Carmen moved along through high school in Chicago and into college.

"We were all—Mother, Father, and I—active in the Spanish-speaking community. There were dances and musical evenings and parties, some sponsored by ethnic groups and some spontaneous.

"One thing was awful. My mother would never let me go out on a date alone. I had no brothers nor cousins in Chicago and my family still followed the old rules of bringing up girls. If I went out in the evening, either my mother or father had to go too. All the other girls could go out with boys on dates. But not me. I didn't like that much. It was painful."

Carmen entered De Paul University in Chicago in 1955, earned both bachelor's and master's degrees there, and then continued for some time with further graduate work at Chicago University and the University of Illinois at Chicago. During part of this time, and later, she was working as an employment counselor with the Migration Division of the Commonwealth of Puerto Rico in Chicago, moving up to being Regional Supervisor of Education and Community Organization. She also organized community action groups on behalf of various self-help programs and developed a Spanish-language curriculum to train police officers, social workers, and teachers to work more comfortably with newly arrived Puerto Ricans.

"The difference of ten years, the ten years which had passed since I arrived on the mainland, was for me more like the span of an age. Now I had a college degree, two of them, in fact. I had two fluent, effective languages. I could open doors, I could do things for people." She also, though she doesn't mention it, had the strong, effective force that had been built into Carmen Maymi working for her.

"There were hundreds of families who needed and were entitled to help, everything from civil rights to welfare, and they not only didn't know how to get these rights, they didn't know they were entitled to them. It was difficult for many of them to comprehend even the simple fact that they were American citizens. I tried to help."

In 1965, Carmen Maymi became Assistant Director of the Montrose Urban Progress Center of the Chicago Committee on Urban Opportunity, and something over a year later she moved into federal service as a Community Services Specialist in the Great Lakes Regional office of the Office of Equal Opportunity. In this post, in 1967, she was named Outstanding Puerto Rican Woman by the Council of Puerto Rican Organizations of the Midwest.

She served three years as project director for a private firm providing assistance to the model cities program, and then, in February, 1972, transferred her activities to the President's Cabinet Committee on Opportunities for the Spanish Speaking, working for Chairman Henry Ramirez, a Mexican-American. In this job she prepared "A Study of Economic Opportunity for the Spanish Speaking in the 1970s" and at the same time evaluated just how effective some ten major federal agencies were in providing opportunities for the Hispanic people. In May, 1972, she became a consultant to the Women's Bureau of the Department of Labor, and six months later the President appointed her director of the bureau. At age thirty-five, she was the youngest woman ever named to the position.

Carmen made her first return visit to Puerto Rico ten years after she had left. Her mother, who is now dead, never went back. Her father did, after eighteen years.

"All my relatives met me at the airport and they looked at me as I walked up to the group. When I broke into

Spanish they were all smiles and laughs and they hugged me. I had been on the mainland for so long they were all afraid I had forgotten how to speak Spanish and had become completely Anglicized. They were all so happy about that."

Carmen lives on Capitol Hill in Washington, not far from the Capitol building, the Senate and House office buildings, the Library of Congress, and the Supreme Court. She has a small house, which she likes and shares with her father and daughter, born in 1963 after a marriage which didn't last long because "it wasn't right for either of us."

She gave her daughter her middle name, Rosa, and they are together a great deal. Rosa goes on many trips with her mother, whenever school time permits. "We are good friends." With Luis Maymi, father and grandfather to his two girls, they are a very close family.

"Though I have lots of outside friends, too, friends of all ages. One of my best friends is a girl fifteen. She reminds me somewhat of myself at that age. And I have older friends, too, of course. They are good friends and good to me. When I was away recently my father became ill. My friends came to the house and took care of him until I could get back."

And Carmen the mother makes a brief return to her daughter. "Did I tell you she is almost as tall as I am? And growing very pretty."

Carmen Maymi follows a pattern that is not uncommon with members of the minorities who have a degree of success; even when they pause for a deep breath to relax, they usually do it with people they actually work beside day to day, or with people who have the same goals.

"I like to swim. I like to walk. I go to the Kennedy

Center and Wolf Trap [theater] fairly often. But mostly I get together with friends. They are usually people who can contribute something. And, yes, they are usually women."

"You prefer the company of women to men?"

"I didn't say that. It depends on a great number of things and these range from mood to timing. Right now I have things to do, things I want to accomplish. I work hard at it and I want people around me who feel the same way. At the moment these happen to be women. And I will probably feel the same way for some time. Marriage is not in my plans at the moment. I have too many things to do."

The scope of Ms. Maymi's operations is rather awesome. She is a member of the Conference of Puerto Rican Women in Washington, serves on the Board of Directors of the U.S. Department of Agriculture Graduate School, on the Advisory Committee for Adult Career Education in Corrections Programs, and on the American Council of Education's Commission on Women in Higher Education.

She also spends about a third of her time on the road, attending meetings, making speeches, at which she excels, flying to California, the Midwest, Texas, Seattle, San Juan, Japan.

"I like talking to people, expressing ideas. It gives one a sense of"—and she hesitated—"I started to say sense of power. But it's more a sense of accomplishment. Or maybe hope of accomplishment."

When Ms. Maymi was named Director of the Women's Bureau of the Department of Labor it was a little like a dream come true.

"I always wanted a job where I could be out in front

fighting for women. Women's rights? It's more than rights; it's the whole place women occupy in the world today."

It may be like the "Ms." she prefers before her name. "When I was nominated for this job the White House wanted a biography. I wrote one and I made it read 'Ms. Maymi.' Someone, probably a man, though I really don't remember, said, 'You can't use Ms. to the President,' and I said, 'I can too' and I did."

In all the speeches Ms. Maymi makes, at all the forums and conferences, discussions and seminars and round tables, she has certain points to make:

"Woman's place is wherever she wants it to be.

"I can foresee a movement of women into the mainstream of society.

"More women of the minorities must join the movement of women into the mainstream."

And she asks such questions as:

"Why don't we have women in the skilled jobs they would be so good at: painting, electrician, cabinet making, air traffic controller, television repair—all kinds of mechanical repairs.

"And maybe some day women will learn that we could make more money repairing that typewriter than sitting behind it.

"There is a word in the Spanish language for the woman who stays at home, cleans the house, cooks the meals and minds the children.

"It is *casera*, literally, one of the house.

"It is time," said Ms. Maymi, "that women stopped being *caseras*. Unless, of course, they really want to be. In that case it's all right."

ROBERTO CLEMENTE
Baseball Superstar

$\mathcal{R}$OBERTO CLEMENTE was a man fiercely proud of being himself. He was a Puerto Rican and a black, and proud of being these things. But primarily he was proud of being Roberto Clemente.

Clemente was a baseball player, one of the greatest in the history of the game. He reached his own particular supremacy in 1971. He concluded a great season that year with an even greater performance in the World Series when the Pittsburgh Pirates won a surprise victory over the Baltimore Orioles, four games to three.

In that series Roberto Clemente hit two home runs, batted a spectacular .414, and time after time established himself as probably the greatest right fielder of all times with his throws to third base, second base, and home plate that, for both accuracy and speed, had never been equaled. In that series the Orioles won the first two games on their own field and the gloom of complete disaster hung heavily over Pittsburgh's Golden Triangle. But the scene then shifted to Pittsburgh, of course, and there the Pirates took the next three straight. By this time, Clemente had already established himself as both the inspirational and physical leader of the Pirates. He refused to lose, refused to be beaten. If there was a momentary slump, he lifted it through pure spiritual force; or with a sharp single and a minute later scoring from first on the next hit by a burst of incredible speed and flying spikes into home plate.

Back in Baltimore for the rest of the series, the Pirates saw the sixth game slip away from them in ten innings. The seventh and deciding game was a classic of contested skill and brilliance. The first score came in the fourth inning when Clemente walked to the plate with two out.

In the bus on the way to the field that morning, someone had read Roberto a piece in a Baltimore paper which had said the Puerto Rican wasn't really a great player. He couldn't pull a ball to left field (Clemente traditionally hit to right) and wasn't really all that good on home runs. Clemente was furious.

"I think," said one of the management staff, "that I feel sorry for the pitcher today."

Clemente usually let the first ball go by. He liked, he said, to get the feel of things. Not this time. He hit the first pitch over the left field wall for a home run. So much for newspaper writers.

The next four innings reverted to a pitchers' battle, with Clemente time after time leading his team in smooth, errorless fielding by his own speed and skills. (Clemente once, not in this series, fielded a bunt from his right field position).

In the eighth inning another Puerto Rican, Clemente's teammate José Antonio Pagan, drove in a second Pirate run with a deep smash against the left center fence, and the Pittsburgh team led by 2-0.

Either score by either Puerto Rican was the margin of victory in the series. In the last of the eighth, Baltimore scored one run and the threat of more had to be snuffed out with fine fielding. The ninth inning was scoreless and when shortstop Jackie Hernandez threw out the last Oriole batter at first, the Pirates went wild. It was only their second World Series victory in forty-five years. Roberto Clemente was named Most Valuable Player of the Series. In the voting by sports writers, no other player even came close.

Highway Three, one of the more important roadways of Puerto Rico, travels eastward from sprawling greater San Juan. About fifteen miles out from famed Morro Castle, it passes through the small city of Carolina, where Roberto Clemente was born, and then continues on through other small and smaller places—Loiza and Rio Grande—and on to the internationally known Luquillo Beach which lies at the foot of El Yunque. This peak, whose name translates in English to "The Anvil," is part of the Sierra de Luquillo range and this in turn is part of the Caribbean National Forest.

The *"barrio"* of Latin America and the Caribbean Islands is often given a fast mental transfer into the English word, "slum." It can be, but is not always. A *barrio* frequently is a solvent neighborhood, kept clean and respectable by the pride of its residents who work hard and earn enough money to feed and clothe their families and maintain the homes, which they usually own, even if on a marginal basis. Barrio San Anton was such a neighborhood in Carolina and there, on August 18, 1934, Roberto Clemente Walker was born. The birthing was accomplished with the assistance of a midwife, as with the rest of the Clemente children.

43

Roberto was the youngest of five children born to Melchor and Luisa Walker Clemente. The mother had been married before and had two children by this union before she was widowed. One, a boy, died in childbirth. The other, Rosa María Oquendo, lived with the Clemente family until she married. (She died later in childbirth.) The other children, in order of birth, were Osvaldo, Justino, Andres, and Ana Iris (who died at age five).

The depression of the 1930s, which gripped the United States, also ruled the economy and thus the lives in Puerto Rico. Most of the sugar farmlands were owned and controlled in the States and the *puertorricaños* who swung their machetes against the cane crops labored in virtual serfdom for barely existence wages.

Roberto's father was a foreman of the sugar workers and thus a cut above them in economic status and entitled to be called Don Melchor by his crew, friends, and neighbors. The Clementes lived in a frame house which, by Barrio San Anton standards, was splendidly large and well set up. It was a pleasant household, too, with lots of love and affection, a friendly place for a small boy with enormous hands and an overweening love of throwing, catching, and batting a baseball to grow up. When he was still a very small child his sister gave him the "little" name of "Momen" which, like so many childish diminutives, had no particular meaning. It stuck with him until he became old enough to demand the use of his rightful "Roberto."

Roberto played in his first organized game of baseball at the age of eight, and by the time he was ten had joined his three elder brothers in the equivalent of today's Little League at the Barrio San Anton school. If his skills at that age weren't great, he more than made up for the lack by a fierce enthusiasm. In high school he excelled at other sports, the four-hundred meter run, the javelin throw, and the high jump, but these were all and always something to occupy his spare time when he wasn't or couldn't be playing baseball.

"I would forget to come home, forget to eat," he remembered later. "I could have played baseball ten hours a day. In fact, some days I probably did."

Throughout his early teens, Roberto played with various amateur leagues in and around San Juan. Then, in 1952, he was scouted by the manager of the Santurce team of the Puerto Rican Winter League, who immediately signed him for a trial season. He received a $400 bonus for signing and a salary of $40 a week.

Puerto Rico had been baseball mad almost from the day the Americans introduced the game and that was via the Spanish-American War "invasion." The Winter League was formed in 1938 with a schedule of seventy-two games played over four months. Many of the players were American professionals, and many of these were black, attracted there for various reasons: the fun of playing, the money, the complete lack of a color line. Their presence gave a high standard of quality to the league's calibre of play but made it very tough for local men to break in.

Roberto had started out at shortstop, but the same powerful arm which had earned him a place there soon sent him out to the field, where he played all three positions at one time or another, ending up, of course, in right field. In his second year with the Santurce team, Clemente found himself playing left field alongside the great Willie Mays who was playing center. Willie coached the eager youngster in the finer points of the game: how to back up a teammate, how to shift with the habits of the batter, to know exactly what you wanted to do with the ball should it come to you.

Clemente was grateful. He idolized the great National League star. But then and forever he was his own man. When later, as it frequently happened, someone compared his style, his great ability, to that of Willie Mays, the Puerto Rican would, completely without offense, respond: "Yes, but I also play like Roberto Clemente."

During these years Roberto was developing the splendid physique (through strenuous exercise, never an alcoholic drink) and the style which was peculiarly his own. He stood five-feet-eleven and weighed 175–180 pounds. His features were finely made and his skin ebony dark. He was a good-looking man. Most notable was the extraordinary pair of hands. They were large and as powerful as the arms which backed them up. Someone once said that Clemente looked like he had on two baseball gloves even when he didn't. It was these hands and arms which gave him the impossible catches—catches made against walls while running in full flight, or sliding on his belly, or even his shoulder—and gave him also the strength and accuracy to throw out base runners from improbable distances. His batting stance was so unorthodox that he fooled pitchers who knew better but simply did not believe that Clemente could stand so far away from the plate and still hit a ball on the far outside. He could hit them from anywhere, and did. Someone once asked Sandy Koufax, the great Dodger pitcher, if he knew an effective way to pitch to Clemente.

46

"Well," said Koufax, "you could roll the ball up."

The Giants' Juan Marichal said: "The trouble with pitching to Clemente is that he can hit anything, strikes or balls. He can hit them off his instep or off his ear. . . . I think he could hit a pitchout."

Clemente played regularly with the Santurce club during the 1953–54 season, hitting a respectable .288 average and beguiling crowds and scouts alike with his fielding performance and the amazing speed and accuracy of his throws. More than half the major leagues in the States made approaches to him during the season, and in February of 1954, he accepted a $10,000 bonus and a salary of $5,000 offered by the Brooklyn Dodgers.

This period was one of transition for the American big leagues. Since the early 1900s they had barred black players, though many of them were demonstrably superior to just about anyone else around. Then in 1947, despite outcries from some of the other clubs, Brooklyn signed the great Jackie Robinson and both leagues were on their way to complete integration—along with a better grade of baseball.

By 1954, when Clemente was signed, the Dodgers already had five Negroes on their roster, four of them regular starters. The fifth was pitcher Don Newcombe. Fearful of having too great a majority of black players on the field at any one time— and, likely, to keep from having to compete against him should he go to another club— Brooklyn acquired Clemente and then assigned him to their International Farm League team in Montreal.

That fall, however, Pittsburgh, which had ended the National League season in last place, drafted Clemente, giving him his first and only home in the American big

47

leagues. The Pirates struggled through the last half of the 1950s, moving up from their cellar position about in direct relationship as Roberto Clemente improved both his fielding and batting techniques. Then, in 1960, they won the National League pennant.

In these years other things had happened to the Puerto Rican star. In October, 1958, he entered the Marine Reserves and spent six months at Parris Island boot camp, emerging as Marine Private Clemente and with certain military obligations which never prevented him from playing baseball. Not long after, actually, his various injuries and ailments barred him from any thought of strenuous active duty. He bought a new home for his parents, establishing them comfortably in a Carolina suburb not far from the place of his own birth. Then on November 14, 1964, he married the girl of his dreams, Vera Christina Zabala.

The tall, eminently lovely Vera was from Carolina also but the two had never met there. Vera attended the University of Puerto Rico three years and then went to work as a secretary. After learning who she was Roberto made one brash direct approach and was rebuffed, and then arranged a meeting through the families. A year later they were married in the Roman Catholic church (though Roberto, like his parents, was a Baptist) which faced the plaza in Carolina. They moved into a home in the Rio Piedras section of the San Juan area. It was rather elegant, with a trophy room, a game room, and an unsurpassed view of San Juan Bay. There also was a nursery which not long thereafter was put to use. The first born was Robertito—junior, of course. Then came Luis Roberto and three years later Enrique Roberto. Someone

48

remarked that he and Vera had produced a "whole outfield."

Life in the United States was never simple for the Puerto Rican. When he first arrived there was a language problem. He had studied English in school, as all Puerto Ricans did, but his command of the tongue was far from conversational. The year in Canada helped but he still used English only awkwardly when he changed his home to Pittsburgh and Forbes Field. Clemente's skin was black and along with other Negro stars of both leagues he was subjected to the discrimination still prevalent in the United States. Often he could not stay in the same hotels with his teammates on road trips, nor eat in the same restaurants. Jim Crow laws were still enforced in the South and Roberto and the other black players suffered the insulting "Go to the back of the bus with the other niggers."

Virtually no sportswriters spoke Spanish, but they thought it highly amusing to reproduce Roberto's accent and his tangled words, often twisting the meaning completely and making him sound and look ridiculous. He thought, and possibly with some reason, that the umpires were not without color bias in their decisions, too. Certainly the records proved that black batters were more often the targets of "bean balls" than were whites.

They even misused his name. Not knowing, nor bothering to learn, that in the Spanish language a son may and frequently does add his mother's name to his father's, they saw Roberto Clemente Walker and assumed it was a mistake. Didn't everyone know his name was Roberto Clemente? They simply wrote it Roberto Walker Clemente so often that the owner finally shrugged his shoulders and let the *gringos* have their own way.

49

And too, there was the trouble of Clemente's injuries and illnesses. He suffered, according to the team records and his own complaints, from—and this is not a complete list—malaria, bone chips in his elbow, a curved spine and numerous loose discs in the spinal column, hematoma of the thigh, insomnia, tension headaches, nervous stomach, pulled muscles, a dangerously strained tendon, and he was frequently actually ill from worrying (about his illnesses, some said). There is no doubt that these various insalubrities were real, as his doctors confirmed, but they were *more real* to Roberto Clemente than they might have been to another man, and he was less reluctant, also, to talk about them. The sportswriters frequently made fun of his ailments and his teammates frequently laughed at them but with good nature, for Clemente would often hold his back or his head and limp on the way to the playing field and then get three hits and be his usual brilliant self in right field. It became axiomatic that the worse Roberto felt the better he would play baseball.

It was probably a combination of all of these things, being black, possessed of a supersensitivity, and his tendency to illness and injury, which prevented Clemente—until 1971—from being acclaimed to the stardom he undoubtedly deserved. Clemente made the hits, the runs, and the brilliant plays, but other men got the headlines. Clemente adored children. He signed and gave away hundreds of baseballs to hundreds of small fans, would always stop and chat with an admirer, loaned out a great deal of money with little thought (or chance) of return, was a good friend and an honorable man, but the feature writers chose other players for their human interest pieces and remembered only Roberto's "Nobody does anything better than me in baseball," which was, after all, pretty close to the truth.

In 1966, he was voted the National League's Most Valuable Player, and in 1970 he hit a thundering .352, but these were only the unattended buildup activities for the year of 1971 and his superlative performance throughout the entire year and then in the World Series. It was that year and that World Series which established Roberto Clemente as the leader of his team, a giant in the world of baseball. *Time* Magazine credited him with winning the Series "all but single-handedly." Two league managers were quoted as judging him "the greatest baseball player I ever saw." and 1971 won him an undoubted place in the Baseball Hall of Fame.

And it made his own world of sports remember that while this was the man who so often moaned as he trotted out to start the game, "Oh, how I hurt, hurt," he was also the man who contributed notable self-effacing humor. As he said on different occasions, "When I wake up in the morning, I pray I am still asleep." And, explaining why he had scored all the way from first on a single, "I had a sore foot and wanted to rest it."

Clemente was, of course, a national hero in Puerto Rico, and only partly for his greatness on the field and in the batting box of the island's national game. He was also a vivid spokesman for the Latin American people as he constantly demonstrated his pride in his race. During the off-season winters on the island, he was tirelessly involved in helping his countrymen, sometimes publicly as leader and spokesman, sometimes anonymously in providing, as he once did, artificial legs for an injured child. He visited Puerto Rican communities in the United States and he used his home in San Juan for countless meetings for charitable activities. The plight of poor children of Puerto Rico worried him and he dreamed of dotting the island with camps, where the emphasis would be on sports quite naturally, and where the boys and girls could get out of the urban and rural *barrios* for at least a time each year. He had other dreams that dwelt with eliminating prejudice and hostility to his land and his people. They all came to an end on New Year's Eve of 1972.

A week earlier an earthquake had struck the city of Managua in Nicaragua and when the awesome devastation was explored, the list of dead reached 6,000 and the injured up to 20,000. Clemente was a willing draftee to head up a Puerto Rican relief drive for the Latin American neighbor and he made it a resounding success. Then, on the night of December 31, Roberto climbed aboard an old DC-7, heavily laden with the food and medicine which had been collected for the earthquake victims. He was leaving his wife and children to watch the New Year in without him because he wanted to see personally that the Puerto Rican shipment reached the proper hands. Aboard the plane also were a pilot, co-pilot, engineer, and five other passengers.

The plane took off, flew out over the ocean for only seconds, and obviously was in trouble. The pilot banked, desperately trying to return to the airport. Then the plane disappeared. It had crashed into the Caribbean. Some of the other bodies were recovered later. Roberto Clemente's was not.

Puerto Rico went into national mourning. A festival marking the inaugural of a new governor was cancelled. On January 14, a final *adiós* was bade to Roberto by the people of Puerto Rico and by many American friends who had come for the occasion. The massive ceremony was held on a baseball diamond which adjoined a new coliseum that had been named for him. On March 20, eleven weeks after his death, the Baseball Writers of America tossed aside a mandatory five-year waiting period and voted Roberto Clemente into the Baseball Hall of Fame, the first Latin American to be so honored. His own epitaph, though, he established in a simple comment after the 1971 World Series.

"I would like," he said, "to be remembered as the type of player I was."

First Latin American to enter Baseball's Hall of Fame, August 6, 1973.

Eleventh man in the 103-year history of major league baseball to achieve 3,000 hits, a mark reached in his last year, 1972.

Most Valuable Player, National League, 1966.

Batting champion, National League, 1961, 1964, 1965, 1967.

Winner of the Golden Glove for fielding excellence, twelve seasons, 1961–1972.

Averaged .317 during his eighteen-year big league career.

Played in twelve Major League All-Star Games, 1960–1972.

Won the Most Valuable Player Award for his play in the 1971 World Series. Tied world record by hitting safely in all fourteen games of the 1960 and 1971 Series.

All-time leader of the Pittsburgh Pirates in games played, at bats, hits, singles, total bases, and runs batted in.

Tied major league record by leading National League in assists for five seasons.

Held National League record with ten base hits in two consecutive games, August 22–23, 1970.

Tied National League record by hitting three triples in one game, September 8, 1958.

LUIS PALÉS MATOS
Poet

LUIS PALÉS MATOS, the "Black Poet of the Antilles," is famous throughout the Spanish-speaking world for his interpretation of the African psyche: its ceremonies and superstitions, its mythology, fears, hopes, dreams, kindnesses, and cruelty. His poems evoke visions of mysterious places and arcane rites. The throb of the drum is always present. Consider his "La Danza Negra":

> Calabó y bambú.
> Bambú y calabó.
> El gran Cocoroco dice: tu-cu-tú.
> La gran Cocoroca dice: to-co-tó.
> Es el sol de hierro que arde en Tombuctú.
> Es la danza negra de Fernando Póo.
> El cerdo en el fango gruñe: pru-pru-prú.
> El sapo en la charca sueña: cro-cro-cró.
> Calabó y bambú.
> Bambú y calabó.

> Rompen los junjunes en furiosa ú.
> Los gongos trepidan con profunda ó.
> Es la raza negra que ondulando va
> En el ritmo gordo del mariyandá.
> Llegan los botucos a la fiesta ya.
> Danza que te danza la negra se da . . .

In English it is "The Black Dance" and the drum throb still comes through.

> Calabó and bamboo.
> Bamboo and calabó.
> The big chief says: tu-cu-tú.
> The chieftainess says: to-co-tó.
> It is the iron sun that burns in Timbuktu.
> It is the black dance of Fernando Po.
> The hog in the mire grunts: pru-pru-prú.
> The frog in the pond sings: cro-cro-cró.
> Calabó and bamboo.
> Bamboo and calabó.
>
> The bodies burst into a furious u.
> The drums tremble with a deep o.
> It is the black race that undulates
> To the lush rhythm of the mariyandá.
> The Botucos arrive at the party now.
> Dancing and dancing the Negress comes forth . . .

Luis Palés Matos was a white man. He was born in 1898, the same year the United States invaded and "liberated" the somewhat surprised and very peaceful island at the conclusion of the Spanish-American War. His birthplace was Guayama, a small town near the southeast coast of the island. It is separated from the remainder of Puerto Rico by the mountain range which lies athwart the island and by the clouds which cling constantly to the summits. Palés loved the nearby sea but the mountains gave him a sense of isolation and probably contributed to the often prophetically melancholy tones of his early poetry. The residents of the Guayama area were predominantly black, and his *nana* or nurse throughout his younger years was a black woman who sang to him and told him stories drawn from a storehouse of African memories. These he never forgot.

His parents came from the middle class but were well educated and their affection for widely varied reading was reflected in what was for the time and place a remarkable library. This love of literature must have been deeply instilled in their son Luis, for he read voraciously in Spanish, French, and English, and began writing almost before he was in his teens. His first book of poetry, *Azaleas*, was written when he was fourteen and published two years later.

In his younger years Palés tried many jobs, principally teaching, but none of them could do anything but get in the way of what he really wanted to do. That, of course, was to write, and write he did, mostly poetry, until his death on February 23, 1959.

Many writers and critics have tried to protest the appellation "black" as applied to Palés' poetry, as did the poet himself: ". . . in my opinion black poetry does not exist, nor white, nor that of any other color. Poetry is an art that does away with color, with fear, with regret."

A Puerto Rican professor, Gustavo Agraít, wrote in 1955: "Even though black poetry has given Palés fame and merit, it also has not been good for him, because many people think that Palés has written only this kind of poetry—black poetry—when the real truth is that the finest of his poetry has nothing to do with the drums, dances, or black skins. I suspect that Palés' poetry is a sincere poetry and not superficial like some of his critics want to infer."

It is more than likely, however, that despite all of the

protests to the contrary, Palés will remain known as "the black poet" although he above all never forgets his origin in Puerto Rico and the Antilles. His first black poem, written in 1918 when he was twenty, was a sonnet, "Danzarina Africana":

Tu belleza es profunda y confortante
como el ron de Jamica, tu belleza
tiene la irrevelada fortaleza
del basalto, la brea y el diamante.

Tu danza es como un tósigo abrasante
de los filtros de la naturaleza
y el deseo te enciende en la cabeza
su pirotecnia roja y detonante.

¡O negra, denza y bárbara! Tu seno
esconde el salmónico veneno.
Y desatas terribles espirales,

cuando alrededor del macho resistente
te revuelves, porosa y absorbente,
como la arena de tus arenales.

The African Dancer

Your beauty is deep, and warms
like Jamaican rum.
Your beauty has the unrevealed fortitude
of basalt, pitch and diamond.

Your dance is like an abrasive grief
which grinds like the roughness
of nature, and desire kindles in your head,
its pyrotechnics red and explosive.

LUIS PALÉS MATOS

Oh! black, dense, and barbarous,
your breast hides the salmonic
poison and loosens terrible spirals,

When around the vigorous male
you turn porous, absorbent
as sands on the beach.

His collection of poems, *Tuntún de Pasa y Grifería* (*Tomtom of Curls and Zambo Kinship*), was written in the years between 1925 and 1933, and of it Dr. Lucy Torres, in her thesis on "The Black Poetry of Luis Palés Matos" for the University of Indiana in 1970, writes:

"Its title suggests the cycle of Negroid poetry contained in it: *tuntún*—deep tomtom, sounds of drums; *pasa, grifería*—the color of skin and kind of hair of the Negro." And, encompassing her entire subject, she goes on: "From the years of *Azaleas* to the last days of his life in 1959, Palés Matos practiced all the techniques of contemporary poetry. One can detect in his works symptoms of neoromanticism and Parnassianism, impressionism, symbolism, modernism, and vanguardism."

Dr. Torres, herself a Puerto Rican and a poet, felt that Palés stressed the equal proportion of the Spanish and the African ingredients of the Antilles, and she thought that he exemplified this in the closing lines of his poem, "Ten con Ten," which translates roughly as "Half and Half":

Y así estás, mi verde antilla,
En un sí es que no es de raza,
En ten con ten de abolengo
Que te hace tan antillana.

59

Al ritmo de los tambores
Tu lindo ten con ten bailas,
Una mitad española
Y otra mitad africana.

      .   .   .

And so you are, my green Antille,
In a way yes, in a way not purely bred,
In a half and half lineage
That makes you so Antillian.
To the rhythm of the drums
You beautiful half and half dancing,
One half Spanish
And the other half African.

After his early years in Guayama, Palés moved to San Juan where he and his family lived in Santurce, a pleasant suburb of the city. He was a short, rather stocky man, neither lean nor fat, dark-haired, light of complexion, almost pink. He wore a mustache and smoked cigarettes. He also drank, "sometimes too much," a friend says.

Except for his interest in literature and writing, he was not a talkative man. When the conversation was to his interest, Palés could sit around a table with friends and colleagues talking and smoking and drinking for hours. But he could also sit there and simply listen when the subject turned to something in which he felt he had little interest and little to contribute. Generally he tended to be more quiet and thoughtful than talkative. He was friendly and on a Sunday morning visit to his relatives in the city would smile and wave to acquaintances or merely neighbors as he walked along the way. He never dressed shabbily but neither did he pay much attention to his clothes. He rather gave the impression he had other more important things on his mind.

Writing came easily to him, friends thought, though they may not have known how many hours he might labor over a line or even a phrase. He was respected, and highly so, in his own time. The latter part of his life he was Writer in Residence at the University of Puerto Rico, one of the many men of great talent brought in by the University president, Jaime Benítez.

Very little of Palés' poetry has been translated into English, or at least translated and published. The most complete collection in Spanish is *Poesia,* issued in 1971 by the Editorial Universitaria of the University of Puerto Rico, with an introduction by Frederico de Onís. De Onís, a Spaniard, was a professor at the university and well known as a writer, particularly as an essayist. He mentions that he was introduced to Palés by José Robles Pazos, another young Spanish professor who later was killed in the Spanish Civil War. In 1927, Robles published an article entitled "Un Poeta Borinqueño" which was the first step toward presenting Palés Matos to the Hispanic world outside of Puerto Rico. The article was very severe, de Onís thought, and "only the black poetry escaped Robles' criticism." De Onís quotes Robles:

"His evocations of mysterious towns—Cambodia, Marousangana, his cannibal dances, with sonorous gong, with *calabó y bambú* and *bambú y calabó*—constitute the most original parts of his work. . . . The base of this composition ("La Danza Negra") is probably in *El Decameron Negro* and in certain French novels of René Maran, Paul Reboux and others." De Onís continues about Palés:

"In 1932–33, a controversy started in Puerto Rico over the authenticity and meaning of the black themes in Palés' poetry. The controversy was not so much over the value of the poetry itself, but over the black aspect of the poetry and its relationship with the Puerto Rican reality and with the ideological content that poetry has to have to be truly representative of a Puerto Rican character.

"Puerto Rican poetry," wrote de Onís, "is and will be national no matter what subject it has, if it is an original poetry and has universal value and at the same time if it has individuality. To identify the Puerto Ricans' or Antilleans' reality with blackness is false. It is like considering the black a stranger to them."

One of Palés' sincerest admirers was Professor Margot Arce, herself a writer and critic of note, as well as a teacher at the University. In 1933 she organized a conference on "Los poemas de Luis Palés Matos" and a few years later contributed a paper about him to the Cuban magazine *Revista Bimestre Cubana* which helped spread the knowledge and esteem in which Palés' work was held throughout the Hispanic world. Of his poetry Margot Arce wrote:

"The poet in his work uses the subjects, the vocabulary and the geography for the description of images. The subjects he uses are descriptions of the towns and customs, the blacks' evocations of the African mythology, rites and superstitions; visions of the landscapes and black geography; satire of the Haiti aristocracy; humorous contrasts between the culture of blacks and whites."

(Some of Palés' critics thought that he was so discontent with his own white culture that he turned to the black because there he found more purity for expression.)

"Palés' vocabulary is heterogeneous. It is composed of words of the Antilles: *ñañigo, baquine, mariyanda, mandingá;* of cries wrenched from the depth of black Africa and which he may have drawn from his own reading: *tungotú, botuco, topé, calibó,* and the *onomatopeyicos* words of Palés' own creation: *coco, cocú, tumcutúm.* He makes abundant mention of the black geography of Tombuctú, Fernando Póo, Martinica, Haiti, the Congo, Angola, Uganda. And the deities of African mythology: Ecué, Changó, Ogún, Bagadrí. And the magic rites, of course.

"He uses the sensuality of sight, touch and hearing. His descriptions suggest almost always visions of sound, color and feeling. These are precise visions. The tonal qualities are reproduced with fidelity."

None of Palés' critics question his rank as a poet, nor the validity of his themes. Nor do they quarrel over what he said in his poetry and how he said it. Their difficulty is classification and identification. Where does he belong?

De Onís, in his very scholarly introduction to *Poesia,* probably comes nearest to an adequate evaluation of the poet and his work; almost certainly that would be true from the viewpoint of the *puertorriqueños* who probably feel as he does without ever defining it. Wrote de Onís: "*La poesia de Palés Matos es española y es negra, y es como la cultura del Caribe, mucho mas. . . .* The poetry of Palés Matos is Spanish, it is black and it is, as is all the Caribbean culture, much more, because the Caribbean is the point of confluence of other cultures with those of northern Europe and the Americans of the United States. The Caribbean is one of the most cosmopolitan and universal areas on this planet, and because of this the poetry of Palés Matos is cosmopolitan and also universal."

HERMAN BADILLO
U.S. Congressman

HERMAN BADILLO remarks once in a while that he really shouldn't be alive today, a reference to the fact that he was born quite literally into the vortex of a tuberculosis epidemic which took the lives of his mother and father and grandmother.

Herman was born in Caguas, Puerto Rico, in 1929, the only child of Francisco and Carmen Rivera Badillo. Caguas is located roughly in the center of the island and had a population of about fifty thousand when Herman was born. By now it has doubled in size.

The Badillos were pretty much in the middle of Puerto Rico's widely spanned class structure. Francisco Badillo was a teacher of English in the public schools and was working on a Spanish-English dictionary when he died at the age of twenty-five. Carmen, the mother, was a cultured, educated woman, active in both church and social work. Her death followed her husband's by five years. In the years which followed, Herman Badillo grew up in the slums of two cultures, not only surviving but thriving in each, and climbing to today's destination.

From that vantage point—the warm, pleasant atmosphere of his offices on Capitol Hill in Washington—Congressman Badillo looks out of the fifth-floor

64

window over the treetops of the city. "I lived in the same room with my mother and father. I was a baby. The disease swept through the whole town. But it never touched me."

The epidemic passed Herman over but he felt its effect in other ways. The death of his parents and his grandmother came in the middle of the great depression which affected Puerto Rico as much and perhaps more than it did the mainland of the United States. He and his grandfather, Eloy Rivera, moved into the home of his Aunt Aurelia Rivera and her two sons, José Luis and Manuel. In age Herman fitted in between his two cousins; José Luis was a year younger and Manuel a year older.

There was no such thing as a regular job for either the aunt or the grandfather; they worked when they could, they scraped and scrounged for food, and they lived in three rooms in a Caguas *barrio,* surrounded by hundreds of neighbors in the identical situation. One of these three rooms was a kitchen. One was a bedroom where Aunt Aurelia and her two sons slept. The third was a room of all purposes—living room, workshop, playroom, dining room, when there was food—and Herman and his grandfather slept there.

The usual diet of the family was rice and beans. Occasionally there was milk. "We never saw meat from one month until the next," said Badillo. "I can't remember a night I didn't go to bed hungry." Welfare didn't exist.

The three boys went to school, where Herman proved himself his father's son by excelling in all his studies and leading his class in high grades every year. And they worked. José Luis got a job helping in the home of the man who owned the neighborhood movie house and was paid in food which he could eat there and sometimes take home. He also got an occasional present of old clothes. Herman worked for the same man in his theater, sweeping out and dusting the seats. In payment for that task all three boys got free admission to the movies, the same films shown in the United States, two or three years removed.

Then, when Herman was eleven, Aunt Aurelia, who still appears as something of an angel to him, acquired enough money to pay the passage of one adult and two children to New York. By this time Señora Rivera had long since ceased to differentiate in any way in her relationship to the three boys. They were not two sons and a nephew; they were her three boys and she thought of them that way, as three sons. Thus, when she had to choose which two of the three to take with her to New York she decided on José Luis, the elder, and Herman instead of Manuel. Her reasoning was basic. Herman was the brighter, the better student; she felt instinctively that he would adapt more easily to a new environment. He would survive. And, perhaps she sensed that Manuel would be happier staying in his native Puerto Rico with his grandfather and other relatives.

In New York, Aunt Aurelia and the boys moved into an even smaller flat in East Harlem, at 102nd Street and Lexington Avenue, in what was to become in time a vast Puerto Rican enclave. It was then April of 1941, thirteen years before Puerto Rico became a Commonwealth, and they were among the first wave of migrants.

"Sure," remembers Badillo, "we knew some English, but it wasn't the same English they spoke in New York and we couldn't remotely carry on a conversation in the

66

language, or understand the teacher. They didn't know what to do with us. So they just put us in a classroom and ignored us, hoping probably that we would go away."

By June when school was out Herman actually did go away. Aunt Aurelia couldn't get regular work and neither could the boys, and the hunger pangs, which were so familiar on the island, were no stranger on upper Lexington Avenue either. Here also were the same living conditions. In Caguas they were called *barrios;* in Harlem they were slums. In either place they spelled misery.

In Chicago, Herman joined another family member, his namesake Uncle Herman, and another American *barrio.* Here the younger Herman sold newspapers and *The Saturday Evening Post* and went to school. He was always a quick learner and by this time was acquiring a facility in English. Thus, when Uncle Herman found himself unable to feed his own family and the additional mouth, too, and shipped the twelve-year-old boy to yet another uncle in Burbank early that fall, Herman was beginning to feel at home in his new language.

That fall was the autumn of 1941, of December 7 and Pearl Harbor and the war, and it brought full employment to Uncle Tomás and the California branch of the Badillo family. Both uncles, incidentally, were brothers of Francisco, young Herman's father, and both had fled Puerto Rico to escape the epidemic of tuberculosis which had virtually wiped out those of the family who remained. Uncle Tomás worked at Lockheed.

Young Herman stayed in Burbank for a year and a half. He attended the Burbank public school. After school and on weekends he delivered the *Burbank News* and soon made enough money to buy a bicycle. Later he

67

also purchased a second-hand lawn mower and it increased his earning power considerably. His grades were always among the highest in his class and his second year in Burbank he was elected president of the eighth grade.

Again, from the Rayburn Building office, Congressman Badillo remembered back more than thirty years. "I could learn anything quickly," he said. "All the textbooks were in English. The teacher spoke only English. In fact, I believe I was the only member of my class who spoke anything else. So I had to learn fast.

"There were a few other Spanish language pupils in the school but I didn't try to cling to them. There was no prejudice there. Kids don't know about prejudice. That comes later and I got into a lot of activities—I was a Boy Scout and went to Sunday School at the Presbyterian church. I made friends easily. It was a happy place for me."

"The Presbyterian church?"

"The Badillo family originally came from Spain to the town of Aguadilla on the Island. The first of them was probably a great-great-grandfather and he and his family had been members of a secret Protestant sect in Spain, secret because being other than Catholic was illegal or close to it at that time in Spain.

"The Badillos were probably the first Protestants in Puerto Rico," the Congressman continued. "That great-great-grandfather is buried in Aguadilla. Not in the cemetery—just outside the gates. Protestantism wasn't exactly illegal on the island, but it wasn't exactly popular either."

Today Congressman Herman Badillo's constituency of some 650,000 in the South Bronx is about 40 per cent Puerto Rican, 40 per cent black and 20 per cent Jewish.

68

"I get along with all of them," he said. Obviously he does just that. In 1970 he was elected to his first term in the United States House of Representatives by 84 per cent of the vote in his district. In 1972 he was re-elected by an 87 per cent majority.

Toward the end of 1944, Aunt Aurelia again prospered to a degree and recalled Herman to New York, where he moved back into her family. They lived in West Harlem, first at 134th Street and Amsterdam Avenue, then at other places nearby. After a year or so Aunt Aurelia acquired an apartment house at 147th Street and Broadway where the group spent the next several years.

Herman first attended junior high school at 127th Street and then moved on up to West Side High School. To his surprise he found himself assigned to a vocational section.

"We spent most of our time learning about one airplane engine," he remembers. "We studied it. We took it apart and we put it together. It was an old standard piston engine and even then I knew that jets were coming. Besides, I wanted to go to college and vocational graduates didn't have the right credits."

So he transferred, with some difficulty, and in 1947 graduated with the highest grades in his class and moved on to City College. In 1951 he graduated *magna cum laude* with a degree in Business Administration. His majors had been in accounting and economics.

"Work? Oh, sure. Work you did because you wanted to eat and to eat you had to have money. Aunt Aurelia couldn't do it all. During high school I worked as a bus boy, pin boy in bowling alleys, dishwasher, waiter. At that time I worked at those jobs part time. In college I worked

69

at the same jobs but it was full time." Classes were attended in the evenings.

From City College he moved on to Brooklyn Law School where, in 1954, he received the First Scholarship Prize, was class Valedictorian, and a member of the *Law Review*. During the years as a law student he worked as an accountant, qualifying in due time as a Certified Public Accountant. Thus, by the latter 1950s, he was both member of the bar and CPA. It was an enviable position for the young Puerto Rican, and add to it the fact that he spoke two languages with no trace of an accent, stood a handsome six feet tall, and was an accomplished, persuasive speaker, both public and private.

In 1955 the young attorney formed, with a friend, the law firm of Permut and Badillo and began a successful practice. He found at that time that being bilingual brought with it certain responsibilities. Several judges, learning of this dual language facility, began calling on him to represent his fellow Puerto Ricans—or any Spanish-speaking defendant—who spoke no or little English, had no funds, but needed help.

He took the cases, of course, and became known throughout the Bronx, where he maintained both his offices and home, as a man generous with his time and talents to help a fellow who needed it. He hadn't lost the ability to make friends easily and he had lots of them. One day it became apparent to him that, surprisingly, he was in politics without having realized it. He joined the Caribe Democratic Club in 1958 and learned the techniques basic to politics: petitions, speeches, the value of personal street-to-street ward work. He also learned about organization and leadership and in these he excelled.

By 1960 he was deeply immersed in what he thought of as an avocation. After all, he was an attorney and he was a CPA, and he could work at either or both. He didn't really need another vocation. But he investigated the John Kennedy organization that year, liked what he found, and joined it. He led the registration drive for his district and had a higher rating than any other. He spoke at rallies and receptions and saw his man elected President.

The Kennedy Club he had worked with turned out to be the most successful in New York and after the election Badillo was instrumental in reorganizing it on a more lasting basis. In 1961 he ran for the post of Club Leader but lost by seventy-five votes and promptly challenged the winning candidate in court. In the meantime, however, Mayor Robert Wagner appointed the rising young Puerto Rican to be Commissioner of the Department of Relocation, which had just been created. He stayed with this post until 1965 and resigned to run successfully for Bronx Borough President in November of that year. His political stature didn't suffer when he was elected a delegate to the 1968 Democratic National Convention (repeating in 1972) nor even by the mayoralty election of 1969 when he sought the Democratic nomination. He lost, but he finished a strong third to two prominent figures who were known city-wide. He tried again in 1973 and finished second.

Then in 1970 he ran for Congress from his district in the South Bronx, was overwhelmingly elected, and became the first Puerto Rican-born man or woman to become a voting member of Congress. (A Resident Commissioner from the Island serves in Congress, representing his people. He can introduce measures, vote in Committee, and speak on the floor of the House of Representatives. But he cannot vote.)

During these years of climbing toward his own goals, Herman Badillo was married twice. The first, in 1948 when he was nineteen, lasted until a divorce in 1960. One son, David, was born to the union in 1956. He was married a second time in 1961 to Irma Deutsch who had two children, Mark and Loren, from a previous marriage. The family lives on West 259th Street. Badillo also maintains an office in the Bronx.

Badillo's district with its more than half million persons is one of the worst urban slum areas in the United States. Many of his constituents are wretchedly poor, many are out of work, many are uneducated. Thus it was natural when their representative moved his political field to Washington in 1970 as a freshman Congressman that he asked for and received a place on the House Committee on Education and Labor. He zeroed in on two specific causes to concentrate on:

• Urban affairs, with an emphasis on the need for low income urban housing.

• The Spanish-speaking people and their problems, including occupational training and bilingual education. Tied in with this was the need for special education for handicapped children.

In the latter field Congressman Badillo in 1973 recruited eighty-eight other members of the House (representing twenty-eight states) to join him in sponsoring legislation which would establish a $55 million home tutoring program for handicapped youngsters. He had researched various state programs and learned that while a few were providing four or five hours a week of instruction for the homebound children, others had paid no attention whatsoever to the problem.

Also in 1973 two amendments he proposed were unanimously adopted by the House Select Labor Committee for the Comprehensive Manpower Act. Both, though couched in legal language, provided that unemployed and underemployed persons who do not speak English as their native language are given particular attention in job training and related aid which will increase their employment and training opportunities.

Nor did the Congressman neglect to relate the amendments to his own city and his own district.

"There is a critical need for bilingual job training in New York," he said, "particularly when you consider the number of persons whose mother tongues—the language most frequently spoken in the home and neighborhood— is other than English." (Forty-eight per cent according to the Census Bureau.)

"These men, women, and children are already being seriously short-changed by many public education programs. We must not also continue to relegate them to second-class status in job training."

The real thrust of Congressman Badillo's dogged energy drive, however, is for a cause he sees even more clearly, one that he can see and touch and smell and listen to every time he walks through his Bronx district— the problem of urban affairs, the plight of the inner city.

Speaking before the Women's National Democratic Club in Washington, he put an hypothesis before his audience:

"Cities are no longer essential to the economic life of our country. They are no longer necessary in terms of our ability to communicate with each other, in order to transport goods and services, or as a concentrated supply of unskilled labor." And, considering his own statement, he continued:

"If this thesis is valid, then it follows that Congress cannot solve the problems of the cities, at least in the sense that cities can never regain their pre-eminence in our economic structure. It would seem then, that if industry flees the cities, taking with it their cultural and professional resources as well, all the people of the cities—rich, middle-class, and poor alike—would likewise leave.

"And if that were the case, our problem would not be a serious one. There would simply be a realignment of our physical environment which would be far more compatible with economic realities and which could lead to a more sensible total way of life for all.

"Unfortunately, this logical replacement is not taking place and it is not about to take place. Instead, the white middle class is leaving the cities while the black, the Latins, the aged, and the poor are left behind. So instead of a logical realignment of our society we have what we now call our urban crisis.

"This crisis stems from the fact that, having decided our cities are no longer essential, we leave them behind and leave with them the unsolved problems of our society. We support, for example, a national policy which does not require that suburban areas provide housing for low-income people—a policy which guarantees the middle class that if it leaves the city, it will not have to take the poor along.

"And this policy guarantees that the cities will become predominantly prisons of the poor, the elderly, and the minorities. The end result is cities that not only are unessential, but undesirable as well because of the array of social problems that persist."

In his office, in Committee, and on the floor of the House, Herman Badillo continues his arguments, all aimed at his major effort to get a measure passed which would create a permanent Committee on Urban Affairs.

"A rural official coming to Washington today," he noted, "can get comprehensive consideration through one Committee alone—the Committee on Agriculture. But if a mayor or other metropolitan spokesman wishes to meet with the appropriate authority on matters of concern to his city, he will have to address his pleas to half a dozen or more Committees and a score of Congressmen. The deterioration of America's inner cities requires a concentrated approach—and it won't happen unless a Committee in Congress is established to do it."

Remembering back over his own upbringing in those inner cities—in his case several of them in two cultures and several degrees of poverty—Badillo said: "Who lures the poor and the uneducated to the cities? I've heard a dozen reasons expressed. My own feeling is that they come because the move represents hope—hope for a better job, better education for their children, a better life.

"And what do we do with them? We let them in and then we lock them in. There is no possible way a poor family man in the Bronx can move into the suburbs or

75

the fresh air of the country. He hasn't the cost of the move, nor the cost of the rent he would have to pay. He is as locked in as if his own particular *barrio* had a twenty-foot wall around it."

Congressman Herman Badillo himself lives in the inner city he talks of, but he managed long ago to find his way through the wall. And now he would like to help those not so fortunate—or self-reliant or ambitious or smart, or all three—to escape also.

CHI CHI RODRIGUEZ
Golfer

CHI CHI RODRIGUEZ has black eyes and brown hair, weighs 120 pounds, and has frequently been compared to a rubber band.

Said Jack Nicklaus, probably the most consistently accurate long driver in the history of the ancient and honorable game of golf, "I get asked many questions about Chi Chi. The most frequent, of course, is whether he can hit a ball as far as I can. The answer is that he certainly has on quite a few occasions. Pound for pound, he must be the longest driver the game has ever known."

Chi Chi is not the most frequent winner on the professional golf tour where he has spent the larger part of the years since 1960, but he has been very consistent in being near the top—among the first five in thirty-five official Professional Golf Association tournaments. By the end of the 1975 season he had won seven titles and approximately $665,000 in prize money.

Many years back Chi Chi set himself a goal of becoming a millionaire. If he isn't there it's because he has given so much away. He has moved a long way from the stark poverty of his childhood when, as he has said, "I was too poor to enjoy just being a 'boy'."

He was born Juan A. Rodriguez Vila on October 23,

1935, in the San Juan suburb of Rio Piedras. His father was also Juan Rodriguez and his mother Modesta Vila Rodriguez. Juan was next to the youngest of six children. There were three sisters, Juanita, Carmen, and Maria, and two brothers, Jesús and Julio.

Juan senior was a plantation worker, which meant that he spent many hours a day swinging a machete at the tough, fibrous stalks of sugar cane which constituted the island's chief, and at that time just about only, industry. Young Juan was one of thousands of *puertorriqueños* who grew up in the *barrios* of San Juan, where everyone in the family worked or scrounged from the age of six in order to contribute anything spendable or edible to the family pot. Young Juan, also like a thousand or more of his compatriots, did a little of everything. He walked the streets selling the peanuts his sisters roasted, he carried water to the cane cutters, he tried going three rounds in boxing preliminaries and didn't like it much. He tried baseball; he tried shoe-shining.

Mostly, though, he caddied at the Berwyn Country Club in San Juan, lugging around golf bags that almost outweighed him. His family had been able, miraculously, to buy a small plot of ground near the club and it was here, in his early teens, that the golf career of Juan Rodriguez began.

Like other small boys in other countries—winning golfer Lee Trevino, for instance—the small wiry Juan had played golf in his back yard, using clubs crudely carved from tree branches, and balls fashioned from battered tin cans and tar, slamming those "balls" back and forth between two holes a hundred yards apart. From this beginning he stepped up his game at Berwyn. He watched the better players and he watched the pro. More, he watched and listened while the pro gave expensive lessons which young Juan absorbed just by using his pair of very sharp ears. And then when the regular golfers had gone home and darkness was only an hour or so away, he could get in a dozen or so holes himself, racing between shots to beat the sun. His clubs were castoffs and the balls so worn and tattered they couldn't be sold as "seconds."

During these same days Juan took a fling at baseball and in fact earned a reputation as a good sandlot pitcher. He also acquired his nickname at this time, adopting for himself the "Chi Chi" of Chi Chi Flores, a popular idol in the San Juan leagues.

But he always returned to golf and at seventeen entered his first tournament, the Puerto Rican Open, under the sponsorship of a Berwyn Club member who had watched the boy hitting balls from the practice tee after work. He came in second in this first competition.

The Rodriguez family had survived their years in the *barrio,* and later too, through the coordinated efforts of every member. The father worked and the children worked and the rewards of their labors were turned over to the mother who managed the household, the family, and the finances, and this was looked upon as a natural thing. Thus when Chi Chi went into the army in 1955 at the age of nineteen and drew his monthly check at Fort Sill, Oklahoma, where he spent both of his two military years, Chi Chi saw nothing strange in the fact that he sent $50 home every month, keeping only $22 for himself.

Chi Chi was popular with his army mates as he is popular on the pro golf tour. He is almost unfailingly good-humored, cheerful, and happy. And he wants to be liked; it is almost a requirement.

"I love people," he has said. "I like being with them, laughing with them, joking. One of the reasons I went on the pro tour was so I could meet a lot of people." There are times on the tour when the Rodriguez romping gets a little too much for his fellow players and they tell him so. Chi Chi is disconsolate for days—sad, despondent. "I can't stand it," he says, and then his conscience-stricken companions relent and their kidding brings him back to the normal happy Chi Chi.

After his stint in the army, Chi Chi returned to Puerto Rico where he worked as an attendant in a hospital for some months and then learned that a new golf course was opening at the Dorado Beach Hotel. Armed with a clipping from his base newspaper at Fort Sill which had carried an account of his triumph in a golf tournament there, Chi Chi duly presented himself to the Dorado pro, Ed Dudley. Fascinated with this miniature man who was lugging a set of women's clubs, Dudley proposed a game. Nervous and pressing, Chi Chi struggled in with a not-too-good eighty-nine score (Dudley was sub-par) but the big pro saw someting in his young opponent that others might not have. "Come back when you're clear of the hospital and I'll give you a try," he said.

The "try" stretched into a number of years during which Chi Chi handled every job in the pro shop, from sales to sweeping out and shagging balls on the practice tee. Dudley gave him what amounted to almost daily lessons and watched as the youngster spent the long hours practicing—driving, chipping, putting, the long irons, short irons, the wedges. And rising young Juan began giving lessons himself and was able to take more and more money home to the family, much to the amazement of his father, who had been vastly disapproving when Chi Chi had dropped out of high school.

Then Ed Dudley left the Dorado Club, to be replaced by another pro who was an off-and-on member of the mainland professional tour. In 1960, under his sponsorship and with some financial help from a wealthy "angel," Chi Chi himself joined the Professional Golf Tour.

The first year he played in twelve tournaments and won a little over two thousand dollars, and in 1961 the result was about the same. In 1963 he jumped to something over $6,000 and publicly credited the switch to a set of men's clubs. Actually it was due more, he will say now, to a change in playing style and to the discovery of his great golf "secret," which is a secret because Chi Chi is probably the only player who can make it work.

He calls it "the solid left wall" and in his book, *Chi Chi's Secrets of Power Golf,* he explains that he had to have more power if, at 120 pounds, he was going to compete against the likes of guys like Jack Nicklaus or Arnold Palmer.

"I learned to build a solid wall of my left side. The theory is that if I have a strong left side and can hit against it, then I can develop a lot of power. This straight wall begins at the top of the left shoulder and continues to the left foot." Chi Chi meant, he said, a straight wall quite literally. He didn't worry about his head or hands, though he was a good enough stylist that these parts probably behaved without any special attention.

Said Dan Jenkins in *Sports Illustrated:* "Imagine a wall,

imagine your left shoulder planted firmly against it, your hip, too, and as much of your leg as you can get into a straight up and down left side. That is the Rodriguez stance."

"Then," said Chi Chi, "I hit against that wall."

Complementing that famous "solid wall" is the equally remarkable Rodriguez backswing. He uses a slow turn, almost a forty-five degree angle, with the body moving laterally off the ball to the right.

"Principally, this increases the distance the clubhead travels on the backswing and gives me the arc of a much bigger man."

The club moves back low to the ground so that on the return the path of the clubhead through the ball is flattened, and this is accomplished additionally by a bending of the knees and turning of the legs.

"When the club has reached the top of the backswing," writes Chi Chi, "I am in a semi-crouch. My left knee has moved well to the right of the ball and I eventually come off my left heel, much more than a bigger man does. This additional leg turn is essential in my swing, allowing me to coil the muscles in my right thigh and reach for the fullest extension possible of the left arm and the muscles of the upper back."

Whatever success anyone else may have with the "solid left wall," it certainly worked for Chi Chi, who now consistently drives from 275 to 300 yards.

In 1963 he won his first PGA tournament, the Denver Open, and that year his earnings totaled more than $17,000. The next year saw him beating veteran Don January in an eighteen-hole playoff to win the Lucky Strike International at San Francisco. Later he defeated

Arnold Palmer by one stroke to win the Western Open at Chicago and was on his way, as a golf professional, despite a badly injured thumb, the casualty of a clubhead caught on a limb in a shot out of the woods. Year after year his earnings continued to be consistently high.

There are basically three kinds of tournaments in which the professionals who make up the Touring Professional Division (TPD) of the Professional Golf Association (PGA) compete. One is the tournament sponsored by a big business corporation, that is, Firestone, Buick, and others. These are usually pro-celebrity tournaments in which the corporation executives and their best customers are paired for the first two days or so with the great names of golf. It's an ego trip for the industrialist, in a manner of speaking, to play with Arnie or Chi Chi or Jack or Lee, and to entertain his friends afterward with first hand reminiscences. And it isn't the worst way to get a decent return from the big bite such an activity takes out of the advertising budget, either.

Second comes the strictly celebrity tournaments, like the Bing Crosby, Bob Hope, Andy Williams, and others. These are "show biz" and almost always charity affairs. The stars of stage, screen, and tube, and those who would like to be, make a contribution to be seen on the networks with the pros. All those big names insure the network and the advertisers of a good audience, and everyone is happy.

In the third category are the institutional tours, those sponsored by individual clubs—the Colonial, Greater Greensboro, Westchester, and the like. When the greatest of the golfers want to drop out for a rest, these are the ones they usually choose to drop out of because the purses may be a little smaller and the television coverage more limited.

And, of course, there is the PGA Tournament, run by the PGA itself, which is made up of the thousands of club professionals over the United States and includes, of course, the members of the TPD as well. The PGA is played all over the country with the pros picking the best course available to them.

And then there are the tournaments in Hawaii and in foreign countries, chiefly the British and the Canadian Opens.

"The tour," where Chi Chi and the other professionals spend a major part of the year, sounds glamorous. Sometimes. Writes Bob Green in *Golf Magazine:* "There's the popular picture of the world-famous golf pro soaring from tournament to tournament in his private jet, playing eighteen with the King of Morocco on Monday, closing a million dollar deal before a dinner date with Raquel Welch on Tuesday, getting in a pro-am round with (fill in your own big name) on Wednesday, hobnobbing with the rich and famous and beautiful at night . . . shooting the record-tying sixty-four score before the national television audience and collecting the $39,000 check on Sunday and winging away."

It sounds great. But it can also be slumps and despair if you're near the top, or just plain despair if you aren't. It can be traveling in a trailer with your wife and four kids, going from motel to motel until they all begin to look alike, the joys of wake-up calls which aren't made, of airline flights canceled, flat tires, lost laundry, and even stolen cars. And of going broke, too, because the tour expenses are high—$15,000 and up a year, and a lot of pros don't make that much.

Life on the tour goes on month after month and for every big winner there are more who strive to make the cut enough times to keep from being kicked off the list. During the course of the year the pro's journeys on the golf route take him close to 100,000 miles. He crisscrosses the United States mainland seven or eight times and the Atlantic and Pacific oceans at least once. Writes Jack Nicklaus in his book, *The Greatest Game of All,* about the time the PGA was played in his then home, Columbus, Ohio: "I spent nine days at home, the longest uninterrupted stretch during the years I had been a pro . . . Over that period I had slowly adjusted to the gypsy life the modern golf pro leads; a new town and a new tournament every week. . . . Through practice I had become a neater packer of suitcases, an authority on steak houses from coast to coast, and a promising geographer." And then, of course, he bought a jet.

Unlike some of the other tournament stars, Chi Chi has never succumbed to the temptations of the private plane to make life on the tour easier. He uses the airlines, the trains, and the highways. Maybe it is with the money he saves in this way that he is able to do the things he always promised himself he would do when he could "earn a lot of money for his big family."

This "family" consists of the dozen or so youngsters he sends to the University of Puerto Rico every year. They include nieces and nephews but they are mostly poor kids who could never make it otherwise. Chi Chi's honest-to-goodness family are his wife, the former Iwalini Lynette

Lum King, an Hawaiian of Polynesian descent, and their daughter Donnette. With them he lives in a very pleasant house that is very near the spot where he used to practice in the back yard with tin cans and tree limb clubs.

In addition to his first three tour wins in 1963 and 1964, Chi Chi's record looks like this:

1965: two seconds, a third, and fourth for $26,567
1966: two seconds, a fifth, and two sixths for $35,615
1967: won Texas Open and total tour winnings of $48,608
1968: won Sahara Invitational plus two seconds for $56,691
1969: one second, other high finishes for $50,726
1970: seven times among the top ten for $53,102
1971: several high placements for $30,390
1972: won Byron Nelson Classic, one second, two thirds, and other high placements for $113,449
1973: won Greater Greensboro Open, other high placements for $91,307
1974: several high placements for $58,940

In 1973, Chi Chi was also a member of the United States Ryder Cup team which won for this country what is about the nearest thing to a world title in team golf. He earned his place on the team with a second place stroke average (71.3) on that year's tour.

It was probably after his first win on the professional tour that Chi Chi told his father that some day he would be a millionaire from the game of golf. Or perhaps it was that he would "make a million dollars" playing golf. With his tour prizes around the $600,000 mark and with the money which teaching, commercial endorsements, and other income his famous name brings, the man who was "too poor to be a boy" probably has achieved his goal. If not, a step he took in 1974 assured that success.

After fifteen years as "head golf man" at the Dorado Beach and Cerromar Beach hotels in San Juan, Chi Chi signed a "multi-year contract" to be Golf Director for Playas de Luquillo, a new condominium complex on the island. Over those "multi-years," this contract alone will bring him a million dollars.

LUIS MUÑOZ RIVERA and
LUIS MUÑOZ MARÍN
Statesmen

$\mathcal{T}$HE MODERN HISTORY of Puerto Rico begins with two men, father and son, Luis Muñoz Rivera and Luis Muñoz Marín.

Muñoz Rivera was a poet, a journalist and editor, a politician and a statesman. He was Puerto Rico's Resident Commissioner, elected in 1910 to represent the island in the United States Congress. His role for his people and homeland has often been compared with that of George Washington and the fledgling thirteen states.

Muñoz Marín, like his father, was an editor and sometimes a poet also, a patriot and a politician. He was the first elected governor of Puerto Rico and chief architect of "Operation Bootstrap," the self-help program which freed the island from its complete dependency on sugar cane and transposed it from a one-crop economy into a multi-industry area.

As alike as they were, and as closely parallel the talents they shared, the men were different, or perhaps it was that the times brought out different facets of their individual endowments. Muñoz Marín, the son, had little need for the militant violence which marked his father's

88

life, the rebellion against hostile authorities and police oppression, and, above all, the cold-steel duels which in his generation must have seemed absurdly archaic. Or perhaps they felt the same and sensed it differently. Muñoz Rivera wrote:

> I was not born to sing pretty songs
> Like a captive nightingale.

His son expressed it another way:

> I have broken the rainbow
> against my heart
> As one breaks a useless sword against a knee.

Muñoz Rivera was born in Barranquitas (which is the name of both a small town and a district of the island) on July 17, 1859, the first of ten boys to grace the lives of his parents. His father was Don Luis Ramón Muñoz Barrios, a merchant and landowner, sometimes mayor. His mother, Doña Monserrate Rivera, presided like the gracious lady she was over the spacious home until the tenth son was born—Luis was twelve—and then quietly retired to a permanent rest from childbearing and other duties of life. She had been pregnant ninety months of the 144 she had lived since Luis' conception. The Muñoz Barrios home is in Barranquitas, in the Cordillera Central, the mountain range which lies across the center of the island. It is only twenty miles from Cerro de Punta, the highest peak in Puerto Rico, and is today a library, museum, and national shrine. Muñoz Rivera is buried in an old cemetery in Barranquitas.

The Puerto Rican schools in the nineteenth century

89

were no further advanced then than other amenities on the island—islanders customarily sent their children back to Spain to complete their educations—and by the time he was ten, young Luis had gone through the local curriculum. His mother, however, had taught him French and his father had an extensive library and supervised a reading program for him which probably did about as good a job of higher learning as an institution of those days would have done. The father also taught Luis bookkeeping. Then, as his brothers came along in maturity, Luis tutored them, one by one, and probably learned through teaching. While his reading program was broad, his favorite subjects were always politics and writing.

Like other young men, his interests bounced around. His first poem, "Adelante," was published in 1882 when he was twenty-three in *El Pueblo,* a newspaper in the city of Ponce. The editor, Mario Braschi, encouraged the young writer, and also urged him to "write about patriotism, not love."

In 1883, he joined the Barranquitas branch of the Liberal Party, thus drawing a raised eyebrow from his father who was a Conservative. (The Conservatives wanted to remain under Spanish rule, though benevolently, they hoped, while the Liberals sought to rule themselves in association with Spain.) In 1884, he opened a general store in Barranquitas in partnership with Quintón Negrón Sanjujo, rather grandly labelled Muñoz & Negrón. It did not prosper. Muñoz Rivera was much more interested in selling political ideas than in selling merchandise. About this time, too, he became president of the local party.

During the next several years Muñoz Rivera found himself becoming recognized both as a political writer and a poet—actually many of his poems were virtually political thoughts, theories, and pleas—and helped put together a new political organization, the Autonomist Party, which was for home rule. The latter action brought down the wrath of both the Governor (appointed from Spain) and the Conservative Party. Since the Governor controlled both local policy and the police, several editors who shared Muñoz Rivera's views were removed from their desks to the barred basement quarters of Morro Castle. One who was not, but who closed down his paper rather than retract or accept censorship, was Ramon Marín, editor of another *El Pueblo,* and who was later to become Muñoz Rivera's father-in-law. Among those jailed, and beaten it was said, was Francisco Cepeda Taborcias, editor of *La Revista de Puerto Rico.* His editorship was offered to Muñoz Rivera, a somewhat precarious honor under the circumstances, but the offer was accepted.

The later years of the nineteenth century were bitterly political on the island. And the political quarrels were frequently punctuated by the duels which, although long-since outlawed in other places, were cheerfully accepted in Puerto Rico as one of the niceties of life. On one occasion Muñoz Rivera challenged a rival politician. The rival refused the challenge and lost all stature in the party. Soon thereafter Muñoz Rivera wrote an article for *La Revista* which enraged the subject, one Vicente Balbás Capó, a Conservative Party leader.

Balbás Capó promptly challenged anyone of *La Revista* to a duel and although he was as poor a swordsman as the challenger was expert, Muñoz Rivera accepted. His second, Dr. José Celso Barbosa, also excelled in the art and promptly informed Balbás Capó that "if Muñoz Rivera falls I will immediately challenge you." The stalwart editor received a slight pinking on the arm, thus satisfying honor without serious physical consequences.

In July of 1890, Muñoz Rivera founded *La Democracia*, the newspaper which was associated with him for the remainder of his life, and later with his son. Three years later he married Amalia Marín in the cathedral at Ponce. Amalia proved a staunch ally for the rest of his career, which meant the rest of his life, and then ably advised her son also.

The object of the political struggles for Muñoz Rivera was, of course, the greatest amount of autonomy he and his followers could wring from Spain. Independence, a complete severing of the ties, was never contemplated seriously, nor was it later in dealing with a new and even heavier-handed master—the United States.

In the latter part of the last decade of the century, Muñoz Rivera headed a delegation to Spain where he came to terms with Práxedes Mateo Sagasta, the perennial head of the Liberal Fusion Party in Spain, and from him won the promise that if he became premier, Puerto Rico would receive a Charter of Autonomy which would in effect make it a province of Spain with all the provincial privileges. In 1897, Sagasta did indeed become premier and he kept his promise. Puerto Rico got its charter.

The Autonomists, led by Muñoz Rivera, became Liberals for Sagasta. Three members of the party, including Muñoz Rivera, were placed on the new Executive Council of six. Muñoz Rivera became Secretary of Grace, Justice and Government and a short time later was named Presi-

Carmen Maymi

Herman Badillo

Roberto Clemente

National Baseball Hall of Fame

Chi Chi Rodriguez

Commonwealth Bureau of Tourism

Luis Muñoz Marín

El Mundo

Luis Muñoz Rivera

Miriam Colón

A production in the park

Pan American Union

Julio Rosado del Valle with one of his paintings

Cóncha Meléndez
El Mundo

Luis Palés Matos
Puerto Rican Information Service

Jaime Benítez

Teodoro Moscoso
Commonwealth Bureau of Tourism

Díaz in costume

Justino Díaz

El Mundo

The Figueroa quintet

Commonwealth Bureau of Tourism

Yvonne Figueroa
and Yosef Yankelev

dent of the Council of Secretaries, which made him for all practical purposes head of the Puerto Rican Government. He was thirty-eight years old, a comparatively tall, somewhat stout man, mustached, a forceful speaker, and a tough fighter. He was known popularly as "The Lion." That was in August of 1897. Less than a year later the United States completed its war with Spain by landing troops on the island whose leaders proclaimed, and probably honestly believed it to be true, that they arrived as liberators. Muñoz Rivera made a valiant attempt to work with the newly installed military government and the ineffective government set up by the Foraker Act, which the United States Congress passed without bothering to ask for help or even suggestions from Puerto Rico. Then he quit and retired to Barranquitas with his first-born son and, among other things, wrote his best-known poem, "Sísifo."

The poem was the story of the Greek legend of Sisyphus, who had been condemned to Hades where his punishment was to roll eternally a huge boulder to the top of a mountain and, as it finally almost reached the peak, to have it slip back down again. In the poem, Sisyphus actually succeeds in reaching the top and then there comes a "slight tremor from the north" (meaning the United States) and again the rock rolls back down. Poor Puerto Rico.

For the next ten years he kept up his never-ending battle for autonomy for Puerto Rico, battling first the military governments and then the appointed civilian heads who followed, fighting to get a better life for his fellow *puertorriqueños* who were virtual serfs on the big American-owned sugar plantations, fighting against the

93

one-crop economy. His newspaper, a new one, *El Diario*, was destroyed by a government-inspired mob and he revived *La Democracia*. Refusing the armed assistance of friends and followers, he was arrested, tried, and acquitted. And with persecution became stronger.

In 1910 he was elected Resident Commissioner, in actuality an elected Congressman with limited powers. He could speak in assembly and serve on Committee. He could not vote on the floor of the House. (Nor can the present Resident Commissioner, though he can vote in Committee.)

He had spent a year learning the English language and now he spent fifteen years using it for the benefit of his fellow islanders. Although his wife and son were there, too, life in what was then a very parochial Washington culture was lonely for him. He was fifty-one. To a friend he wrote: "I am here alone in a tomb-like isolation, mixing with people who speak a different tongue, who have no affinity for my way of life, who are not hostile, who have no real interest but are indifferent and cold . . . as the granite stones which support their big capitol."

In Washington he worked indefatigably to make an impression on an officialdom that must have seemed like a featherbed of indifference. Nobody opposed, but then, nobody supported, either. But as the years went on, Muñoz Rivera made impressive friends, men like fellow-intellectuals Woodrow Wilson, who became President of the United States in 1912, and Henry L. Stimson in the Cabinet, and Felix Frankfurter who was later to serve on the Supreme Court. And he managed to impress some members of Congress to the extent that, in 1916, Congressman William A. Jones, a Democrat from Virginia, introduced a measure which would grant full citizenship to all Puerto Ricans and which instantly became known on the island as "El Bill Jones." Muñoz Rivera campaigned for it with a terrible intensity. He talked to fellow congressmen, swung every ounce of persuasion he could mount on every senator he knew. He pleaded its case with President Wilson. On March 17, 1917, it was signed into law. Muñoz Rivera had died the previous September, but it was his triumph, nevertheless.

Seven months after his father's death, Muñoz Marín wrote that he had inherited a great name but that he did not intend to be a copy of his father. Actually, it was twenty years before he sought and accomplished political leadership and success.

For the first two years after his father's death, Muñoz Marín served in Washington as secretary to his successor. In a way, returning to the United States was like going home. He had been three when his family first lived in New York and he had been in Washington in school during his father's service there as Resident Commissioner. He also wrote continuously—poetry for *La Democracia,* which explained, or tried to, the oddities of life and outlook on the mainland.

"The American people are really tolerant and generous," he wrote. "They love liberty and, while they don't go around shouting about it these days, they appreciate liberty." Like his father, Muñoz Marín must have wondered what he could ever do to extend this feeling to the island of Puerto Rico.

After the labor of collecting and publishing his father's writings, he started, in 1918, a new newspaper, *La Revista de Indias* (*Review of the Indies*). His idol in the world of writing was Edwin Markham, the American poet, and Muñoz Marín, after visiting and becoming friends with Markham, translated his best-known poem, "The Man With the Hoe," into Spanish.

In the latter 1920s Muñoz Marín moved his *La Revista* to San Juan, joined the Socialist Party, and became active in political affairs. Meantime he had married Muna Lee, a native of the mainland, who gave him two children. During these years Muñoz Marín was in and out of political action, usually disillusioned, in and out of editorships, always writing, and beginning to pick up the battle against poverty and subjugation that had occupied his father for so long.

During the years since Puerto Rico became a possession of the United States prosperity of a sort had resulted for the island, but the prosperity for the *puertorriqueños* might be compared to that of the slaves on the antebellum Southern plantations. They didn't starve or freeze.

The production of sugar cane on the island had multiplied sevenfold since 1898 when the *americanos* marched in, and so had its value. Little of the money, however, benefited Puerto Rico, for the sugar cane lands were owned almost entirely by big mainland companies which hired cheap labor, skimmed off handsome profits, and reinvested the money elsewhere. The island found itself virtually one big plantation, with the workers held in virtual serfdom by methods that were proven, traditional, and cruelly effective; they were bound to the land and the job by debts—debts they could never pay off nor escape from. Many companies even paid in script which

96

was only good at their own company stores or for the rent of squalid company houses.

Muñoz Marín fought the battle of Puerto Rico through the depression of the thirties, helped organize help for the thousands of hungry on his island, and found a glimmer of hope in the policies and actions of Franklin D. Roosevelt when he was elected President in 1932. Then, in 1937, at the age of forty and supremely disgusted with the politics of the island, he began a major life work, the organization of a new political party, El Partido Popular Democrático.

The emblem of Los Populares was a man wearing a big straw hat. The hat had obviously been woven by hand and the wearer was a farm worker. The legend below gave the new party's philosophy in just three words— Pan—Tierra—Libertad. Bread, land, and liberty were the things Muñoz Marín wanted most for his island. He campaigned incessantly and he convinced the farm workers, the *jíbaros,* most of whom had been selling their votes for the traditional two dollars, to "lend" these votes to him instead and he would return the loan with benefits of far greater value.

In the first election, in 1940, Los Populares won an amazing ten out of nineteen seats in the Senate and eighteen out of thirty-nine in House. Muñoz Marín was elected President of the Senate. Only months later World War II started and Washington became too busy to pay much attention to its small offshore possession, except as it affected the war, which it did in two ways. One was a chore: patrolling the water between the island and the mainland to block out German subs. But on the other side of the coin were the thousands of young *puertorriqueños* who either enlisted or were drafted into the armed forces.

Under Muñoz Marín some things were accomplished on the island itself, chiefly a new income tax which was better enforced. And there were echoes of the Roosevelt New Deal in various new agencies—a Minimum Wage Commission, a Government Development Bank, and a Planning Board for Puerto Rico.

The 1944 elections brought a clear majority for Muñoz Marín's Populares, with seventeen out of the nineteen seats in the Senate and thirty-seven of the thirty-nine seats in the House. Now he could move toward both agrarian and wage reforms. An old law, never enforced, limited land ownership to five hundred acres, and the government served notice on the superlandowners by taking over some 120,000 acres and placing them under the ageis of the new Land Authority. The Authority established wage minimums and hour maximums for itself and the private landowners had to follow suit. New villages were established and thousands of families moved into them, with surrounding land to cultivate. Hospitals were built. Schools were established and teaching was in Spanish again, not absurdly in English which the teachers couldn't speak nor the pupils understand (as it had been for years).

During many of these turbulent years for the new government, their greatest ally was the first *simpático* governor the island had ever had—President Roosevelt's appointee, Rexford Guy Tugwell, who served from 1941 to 1946. In later years, after retirement, Rex Tugwell wrote of the "great" political leaders it had been his privilege to work with; Franklin D. Roosevelt was one and Luis Muñoz Marín another. He not only backed Muñoz Marín as governor, but it was probably his influence in 1947 combined with the island progress under Muñoz Marín's Senate leadership, which had led the American Congress to enact the law which provided that Puerto Ricans should freely nominate and elect their own governors henceforth; and three years later, in 1950, to pass Public Law 600 which suggested that Puerto Rico draw up a new constitution and reorganize its government.

Thus, after more than fifty years of unending battle for autonomy, Puerto Rico became a Commonwealth of the United States. Residents remained citizens, economic ties became closer, and those of business held out great promise.

Those promises began fulfillment with the formation of "Operation Bootstrap" which brought the boom of industrial development and an unprecedented tourist trade to the island. The man responsible for the new flood of prosperity, was Muñoz Marín's protégé, Teodoro Moscoso.

The election and re-election of Muñoz Marín as governor became so habitual that his action in stepping down in 1964, as he was approaching the age of seventy, came as a personal shock to the islanders, who found it difficult to accept this lesson in democracy.

"No man should be in power too long," he told them.

However, he did return to the Senate, where he continued to serve the cause of Puerto Rico.

TEODORO MOSCOSO
Economic Planner and Developer

In 1950, Governor Luis Muñoz Marín appointed a demonstrably bright, innovative, and effective young island businessman named Teodoro Moscoso to be administrator of the Economic Development Administration of Puerto Rico, better known as Fomento, and asked him to launch "Operation Bootstrap."

Fomento translates best into the word "promotion" as it is understood in today's business world. And "bootstrap," of course, refers to the old adage which counsels lifting oneself by one's own bootstraps. Moscoso held the post for ten years with phenomenal success.

Twenty-three years after the original appointment, another Governor, Rafael Hernández Colón, in 1973, called him back to the same post, a summons which he accepted. In the intervening years he served two United States Presidents as Ambassador to Venezuela, Coordinator of the Alliance for Progress, and U.S. Representative on the Inter-American Committee of the Alliance.

Ted Moscoso was born in Barcelona, Spain, but grew up in Ponce, Puerto Rico, and passed his early years confident that he would enter the family drug business, but it didn't work out that way.

Very soon after graduating from the University of

100

Michigan, he found politics, or at least public service, more interesting than pharmacy (although he had worked well in the business). He also demonstrated a remarkable aptitude for deftly finding paths through both indifference and red tape to get things done. From 1938 to 1942 he was Vice Chairman and Executive Director of the Ponce Housing Authority and guided it through the building of several hundred units of low-cost housing. He got his training for Fomento as head of the Puerto Rico Development Company (PRIDCO), a government agency with a capitalization of $25,000,000. With the backing of Governor Rexford Tugwell and Senate leader Muñoz Marín, he and PRIDCO began taking over unprofitable but promising factories and moving them from the red into the black. He touted them as pilot plants and eventually had a couple of dozen going with a total production of about $25,000,000 and an annual payroll nearing $4,000,000.

Then, recognizing as others hadn't that two of Puerto Rico's greatest assets, the climate and the beaches, both beautiful, were marketable, his PRIDCO launched "Moscoso's Folly," a big, swanky, expensive resort hotel in the Condado section of the city, and then leased the $6,500,000 structure to Conrad Hilton. It became the Caribe Hilton, a bit of a hostelarian gold mine. It also signalled the beginning of a multimillion-dollar tourist trade for the island.

In 1950, Muñoz Marín became the first elected governor of the island and promptly advanced the concept of PRIDCO into the concept of Fomento. Dangling the carrot of a twelve-year exemption from real estate and income taxes, plus a virtually unlimited labor market at low wages, plus government help in financing, not to mention the pleasure of living in this heavenly climate which the airlines had brought only a few hours from New York, Ted Moscoso grabbed the Fomento project and ran; it succeeded beyond the originators' maddest dreams.

Typical of Moscoso's operations in those early days of "Operation Bootstrap" is the story of an incident which occurred when he was on a train from New England to New York. He met Businessman One he had known before, who introduced him to Businessman Two, and the three of them went into the club car for a drink. Businessman Two was vocal in his complaints about the problems of his company in Providence—the difficulty of finding workers, the mounting payroll costs, the frictions between labor and management, higher taxes—all of the woes inherent with capital.

Moscoso listened and then he mentioned his own isle, and its tax incentives, its accessibility, its ready labor force; and he mentioned wages which were from one-third to half lower than those on the mainland. And mentioned, too, that it flew the American flag and its products went duty free across the waters to the markets of the mainland.

Among the other lamentable woes of Mr. Two's corporation was a considerable profit which had piled up and which the management would like to use for expansion rather than pay out in taxes.

So the conversation continued in New York the next day with other officials of the company. A few days later they all went to Puerto Rico and a few days after that signed an agreement which resulted in a $1,600,000 factory which would employ some five hundred persons and generate a payroll of more than $4,300,000 annually.

There are dozens of similar stories: the man who dropped into Moscoso's office in San Juan and told him, dead-pan, "I'm sorry but I'm afraid our Crane China Corporation can't operate in Vega Baja."

Moscoso was concerned and puzzled. "Why not?"

"Not enough people who want to work."

Moscoso was incredulous. "Not enough people? I can't believe it."

"Yep," came the reply. "We advertised that we wanted about twenty girls that we could train to decorate dinnerware as a task force for the four hundred or so we'll need when we get into full operation.

"The next morning only 1,000 showed up."

Vega Baja is about twenty-five miles or so from San Juan and the same from Arecibo. Many of the applicants had come from each place, traveling twenty-five miles from their homes to hunt work.

In the first twenty years of PRIDCO and "Bootstrap," Moscoso and Governor Muñoz Marín carried the message throughout the United States (and elsewhere) of the industrial paradise that was Puerto Rico so well that more than 700 new plants were established there. Unemployment vitually disappeared and per capita income rose to standards which, for the island, represented a fair degree of prosperity. And the Americanization of the island continued until it became an embarrassment to those Puerto Ricans who were concerned about the bastardization of the language, the customs, the arts, and who were interested in maintaining a reasonable degree of the graceful old Spanish culture.

His job must have seemed finished to Teodoro Mos-

103

coso at the end of those twenty years in 1962. So he entered another field of public service, this time for another government, the United States.

Moscoso has been described by admiring mainland writers as a Puerto Rican with Yankee drive, a phrase obviously intended to be complimentary. A better description might be that he was always intelligent, innovative, competent—a salesman with a good product, a man who could get things done.

He was born José Teodoro Moscoso Mora Rodríguez on November 26, 1910, in Barcelona, Spain, the son of Teodoro Moscoso Rodríguez and Alejandrina Mora Fajardo. His father was a pharmacist and his mother had long been active in civic and religious affairs. Both were American citizens. There were also a brother and a sister, José Guillermo Moscoso and Carmen Leonor Moscoso de Cintrón.

Young Teodoro was still a child when his father returned with his family to Ponce where he had established a drug business in 1898. The things which interested Teodoro were demonstrated in high school. He was elected president of his senior class and was captain of the school debating team. Fully anticipating that he would work in the family business, Teodoro's father enrolled him in the Philadelphia College of Pharmacy where he was editor of the school publication, *The Scope,* and where he won a scholarship which took him to the University of Michigan at Ann Arbor. He graduated with a Bachelor of Science degree in 1932 after majoring in chemistry. He had been assistant editor of the school magazine, *Gargoyle.*

Back in Ponce, Moscoso became general manager of

the retail side of Moscoso Hno. & Co., Inc., and a little later president of the wholesale division also, remaining with his father until 1939. He had been, for several years, interested in low-cost housing and in 1939 became a member of the municipal housing authority of Ponce. For two years he read and studied everything he could get his hands on about the problem, working his way first into the vice chairmanship of the authority and then later becoming executive director.

Moscoso was a young man in these last days of the Great Depression, still in his late twenties. He stood nearly six feet tall and weighed about 185, a man who may have worried a little about his already thinning black hair. He was softly and deceptively persuasive in two languages, his English touched with only the faintest of accents. His friends knew him as Ted or Teddy. On the mainland he was a Democrat and on the island a member of Muñoz Marín's Populares. His working day was often double the normal eight hours but when he found time he would turn to painting, music, reading (Marcel Proust his favorite) to pause for a long breath. He was married on July 3, 1937, to Gloria Sánchez Vilella. They have one son, José Teodoro, and a daughter, Margarita.

Moscoso's housing operations in Ponce by 1942 had attracted so much attention throughout all Puerto Rico that Governor Tugwell named him administrator for the entire island.

Public housing was fine, and Moscoso directed the building of five huge projects throughout the island, but he knew—as did Tugwell and Luis Muñoz Marín, then President of the Senate—that housing was a panacea, an aspirin for the ills which went to the heart of Puerto

Rico's poverty. Until the island could be freed from its dependency on one major product, sugar cane, and two minor products, coffee and tobacco, it would remain just a poverty-stricken nonentity. So, from the discussions the three men had about the problem, Moscoso wrote the legislation which produced PRIDCO and later Fomento.

Their success, plus Muñoz Marín's taming of the big sugar corporations, was history on March 29, 1961, when President John F. Kennedy named Moscoso United States Ambassador to Venezuela, the first *puertorriqueño* ever to be named to an ambassadorial position. It was a job which required a degree of diplomatic skill which Moscoso either possessed or acquired. A general sentiment of violent anti-North Americanism prevailed throughout the country and was particularly strong at the Central University in Caracas. The students demonstrated when Moscoso arrived and when he visited the campus a month later they burned his car. To a group of them who regretted the incident and apologized to him later, Moscoso said thanks, but passed it off with a Latin shrug. "I have felt the urge to do about the same thing on occasions," he told them.

Some eight months later, on November 6, President Kennedy moved Moscoso up from his Venezuela post to be United States Coordinator of the Alliance for Progress and assistant administrator for Latin America in the Agency for International Development (AID). This gave him rank equal to that of an assistant Secretary of State and required Senate confirmation, which came along early in 1962. The Alliance and AID were closely related and in turn worked through the Organization of American States (OAS), which was Moscoso's next destination when, on June 3, 1963 President Kennedy named him United States representative on the Inter-American Economic and Social Council of the OAS.

It was a job a man of his talents could not enjoy very much. He was constantly frustrated by what he considered a lack of solid achievement by the organization. His own chief accomplishment was the formation of a thirteen-member Latin-American Science Board. It was intended to advise the Alliance for Progress on making more effective use of technology and of science in helping alleviate poverty, covering such areas as housing units, school classrooms, wells and water systems, textbooks, farm credit, small business loans, and the actual distribution of food stocks. During the years of his work with the various agencies dealing with Latin America he traveled throughout the United States and in the Latin-American countries, of course, explaining the meaning and purpose of the Alliance. He also wrote for newspapers and magazines, even for encyclopedias.

In 1964 he gave up government service, resigning to take the position of chairman of the Executive Committee of the Banco de Ponce, although he later also served as one of six Puerto Rican members of the Joint United States-Puerto Rican Status Commission which had been created by Congress. And in 1964, President Lyndon Johnson named him one of the sixteen members of the President's Panel of Consultants, a group formed to advise the chief executive on foreign policy. In February of 1966 he became chairman of the Board of Directors of Commonwealth Oil Refining Company.

And then in 1973, Governor Rafael Hernández Colón called him back to head Fomento once again. It must have been one government job he could accept with some pleasure. At Fomento, he knew, he could get things accomplished whatever he decided they should be.

MIRIAM COLÓN
Actress

$\mathcal{M}$IRIAM COLÓN is the most notable Puerto Rican actress in America, the most accomplished and probably the most famous. She has starred in more than two hundred television shows, has been featured on Broadway, and has screen credits by the score, including supporting parts in *One-Eyed Jacks* and *The Appaloosa* with Marlon Brando, and *The Possession of Joel Delano* with Shirley MacLaine.

More important, though, she is the founder of the Puerto Rican National Theater and the energy force behind its successful operation. Patricia Bosworth writes of the theater's traveling unit in *The New York Times:* "From every corner of the block on 110th Street in East Harlem they came to see the Puerto Rican Traveling Theater and those who couldn't hung out of apartment windows and watched as technicians assembled the portable set. . . . Teen-age mothers moving forward in little giggling clusters while their husbands lolled against the parked cars. Old people. Kids careening around on bikes.

"In the midst of the noise that evening stood actress Miriam Colón, the executive director. A tiny woman with long dark hair and flashing eyes, her face radiated intense concentration as she met with community leaders and signed autographs for some black students who asked her questions about Hollywood."

The formation of the Puerto Rican National Theater traces back to 1967 and *The Oxcart,* in which Miriam Colón played one of the leads in an off-Broadway production at the Greenwich Village Mews Theater and which ran three months. *Oxcart* was written by Rene Marques, a Puerto Rican playwright, and it takes a Puerto Rican family, actually *jíbaros,* poor mountain farmers, from the rural poverty (Act I) to a *barrio* in San Juan (Act II) to a New York slum (Act III).

"I first saw the play performed in a church basement twenty years ago," said Miss Colón. "The play is revealing in its portrayal of how one family fights its problems through the three separate environments. It has a tremendous impact.

"When I wanted to produce it in New York most of my friends said I was crazy. 'It's a play about Puerto Ricans,' they said, 'This is New York.' But I felt its appeal was universal. It was a story of a family trying to survive.

"The play has several leads. I played the part of Juanita, a young woman. The play turned out to be very successful. The audiences were black, white, Puerto Rican, Mexican—everyone. If you had ever known poverty you could relate to it."

Sponsored by the city's Summer Task Force, *Oxcart* toured the city in 1967, playing in parks, on church steps, store fronts, and even in jails. And from that beginning evolved the Puerto Rican National Theater, a nonprofit, all-professional organization with three divisions: the traveling unit, a laboratory and training unit, and a class for chorus singing. It is supported by foundations, the New York state and city governments, and anyone else

Miriam Colón can wheedle a dollar out of.

Miriam's own acting career began when she was thirteen and in junior high school. She was cast as the lead in the school production of *La Azotea,* (*The Roof*) by Alvarez Quintero.

"I loved it. I knew right then there could never be anything as important for me as the stage."

Miriam was born in the city of Ponce, to Teodoro Colón and Josefa Quiles. Her mother and father were divorced when Miriam was little more than a baby. Both parents married again and had other children, so Miriam grew up with an assortment of half brothers and sisters—Jorge, Tein, Ruben, Onelia, and Dolly—as she shuffled her life between her mother and father.

"It was very confusing. It was not a happy childhood," she remembers, looking back. "We never lived in *barrios* exactly. We were always in little houses of one kind or another. But we were a long ways from being well off."

The man who directed Miriam in her first play was a professional actor and his work with the high school production was a project for the Department of Drama at the University of Puerto Rico. He was impressed by Miriam's potential as an actress and, perhaps more, by her enthusiasm and her eagerness to study and learn more about acting and the stage. He told the head of the Drama Department about his protégé and she was given permission to audit evening classes as an observer.

She was at that time living with her father in Santurce, a San Juan suburb near Rio Piedras, another suburb where the University is located. For several years thereafter, while she completed high school, Miriam would catch a bus in Santurce after school and ride to Rio Piedras where she would sit in on classes which might last two or three hours, watching, listening, absorbing, soaking up the arts and techniques and lore of the theater. Dinner went by the board until she got home at nine or ten o'clock for whatever might be left over from the family meal.

She played in her first "professional" production when she was fifteen after being permitted to read for a part in a play produced by the Drama Department, *Milagro de San Antonio.*

"I got the part. I played a deaf old lady and had six lines. To me that was more a miracle than the *milagro* of the title."

From this small beginning Miriam went on to bigger parts and then to a permanent role in the University's traveling theater which played anywhere it could on the road—schools, squares, bandstands, any open area.

"I was delighted. I had never been anywhere and I loved to travel. I got to meet people. But best of all, I got to act and I had a taste of applause. I loved that, too. The first play I toured with was *La Zapatera Prodigiosa (The Shoemaker's Prodigious Wife)* by Fredrico Garcia Lorca."

The first roles were small but they grew bigger.

"We played Lenomand, Ibsen, Shakespeare, Chekhov, Socrates—plays by a dozen writers. It was basic training, but it was also graduate work. And during the course of it I became well known to Puerto Rican audiences. I guess I even achieved a certain popularity."

And then she graduated from high school and it was time to go to the University.

"I was nineteen. I didn't want to study anything except drama, of course. But I had had all of this experience. In a way I was a fairly seasoned actress. I couldn't very well enroll at the University and take Acting One."

If Miriam was a special problem for the University, the officials there also realized that she was a special talent, too, and in conjunction with the Resident Commissioner in Washington, a special scholarship was set up and Miriam went off to new studies and a new life in New York City. The scholarship was at the Dramatic Workshop and Technical Institute on Broadway.

Miriam was at the Workshop for two years and then, at the age of twenty-one, she auditioned for admittance to Elia Kazan's Actor's Studio, a foundation-supported "graduate" school of the theater. For her first tryout she prepared a five-minute scene from Lorca's *Blood Wedding.*

"It is a very dramatic scene—a scene between the bride and her ex-boy friend who is now married. I chose it because it suited my age range and, also, my dramatic range. I played it straight."

She passed the audition and was admitted conditionally but had to pass a second test and this time chose a bit from *Marco Millions* by Eugene O'Neill. It was a very short scene between a young Chinese princess and her father.

"It was a very important audition for me, of course. For some reason the first one hadn't bothered me but this one did. I was sick all day—headache, upset stomach. I almost didn't make it."

But she did, and was admitted. Miriam's mother had come with her to New York and had found work as a seamstress in the garment district. She and Miriam lived in a tiny one-room flat on West 25th Street. The Studio was free to the students and ran ten months a year with classes in acting, dancing, singing, speech—all of the theater arts. Miriam stayed there several years, studying and working, trying for and frequently getting any acting parts that might come along in any theater or any theater medium. She also got involved in an early marriage which lasted eighteen months.

"Too young," said Miriam. "And too quick. It was wrong for us both."

Then she tried for and won a Broadway role in *The Summer House* with Judith Anderson and that was the giant step which started her on the pleasant road to recognition and a score of better acting jobs. In 1956 she had a featured role in the off-Broadway hit, *Me Candido,* and when it closed she went to Hollywood to play the same part at the Players Ring Gallery.

She stayed in California seven years, during which time she had parts in just about every major network series show ("God, did I get tired of playing sad-eyed Spanish girls") and worked in films with Brando. That was different.

"In the films with him—both of them—I had parts which were not stereotyped. I wasn't betrayed or even left behind by a heroic lover. I had parts which demanded spirit and action. And Brando is a remarkable man to work with, very sensitive to every detail, both in acting and directing."

Although she made money in California and liked it after a fashion, Miriam knew after seven years that she had stayed long enough. And then, on one of the many trips back to New York which she made periodically, she was introduced to George P. Edgar, a securities analyst. This time Miriam waited two years to be sure and then was. They were married on April 24, 1966.

Today the Edgars live in a big triplex town house on West 94th street in New York, between Columbus and New Amsterdam Avenues. The entrance is on the English basement level and a short hallway leads to a dining room usually cluttered with scripts or bits of script or just papers in general. Through the dining room is a pleasant garden. There are two apple trees that bear fruit, azaleas and other shrubs, dozens of potted plants bordering a flagstoned plot of garden chairs, lounges, and a table. And two Siamese cats.

They are Mr. Tiny and Mr. Tim, seal points, brothers from the same litter, vintage 1970, and virtually indistinguishable. When Miriam sat down, one of them immediately jumped in her lap.

"This is Mr. Tiny," said the actress. "He's very affectionate. Likes people. Mr. Tim"—waving to the other Siamese who had settled on the table—"is more reticent. He's concerned with nature, trees, butterflies. And he also guards against other cats.

"We used to have one rather constant visitor, a big blonde we called Jean Harlow. She was very forward. She would go into the kitchen and mop up all the food from the cat dishes. So Tim jumped on her one day and drove her away. I was sorry because she was a very pretty girl. But Mr. Tim thought she had carried things too far."

At this point Mr. Tim, the cat who didn't like people, jumped down from the table, strolled over to a visitor, put one tentative paw on his knee, then jumped into his lap and settled down. He and Miriam looked at each other. She shrugged. It was Latin and expressive.

"And," she said, "so much for type casting." Mr. Tim

115

stayed in the lap for the next hour and a half.

It was the experience with the University of Puerto Rico traveling unit, of course, which inspired Miriam to put *Oxcart* on the road, if touring New York City can be called that. "On the streets" is the more descriptive phrase she uses. Her first money for the venture came from then Mayor John Lindsay and her record has been one of continued success.

The performances would probably horrify a traditional actor, accustomed to traditional audiences. After experimenting with seats for the watchers, Miriam left the audience standing because they preferred it. During the performance they mill about, talking over the dialogue; they walk away and return. "That's the influence of television. Remember, many of the people watching have never seen any other live show."

The traveling theater also has its dedicated fans who follow it from one part of the city to another, turning up night after night. They get to know the lines and sometimes repeat them aloud with the actors.

One night a woman, who had obviously seen the show time and time before, became so carried away during a scene depicting protesters and police that she leaped on the stage and joined in the dialogue. The performers, who are accustomed to just about every kind of distraction, simply ad-libbed her into the scene and went along until the woman finally wandered off the stage. Most of the audience probably weren't aware that anything odd was going on.

The shows which Miriam produces, and frequntly acts in, range from farce to drama; they are always professional. Writing in the New York *Daily News* about two

116

MIRIAM COLÓN

state-supported theater units and their back-to-back performances, Tom McMorrow panned one mercilessly and
then wrote about the other. "A far happier use of the
state's funds can be seen in the performances of *The Pas-
sion of Antigona Perez* by the Puerto Rican Traveling Theater. The English-language production of the old Socrates classic by Puerto Rican playright Luis Rafael
Sanchez transforms the tyrant Creon into the person of a
Latin-American military dictator. Miriam Colón, founder
of this admirable company, is Antigona, and Manu
Tupou, who just two weeks ago was on Broadway with
Ingrid Berman in *Captain Brassbound's Conversion,* is the
generalissimo.

"They are topnotch actors and the direction . . . set-
tings, lighting, and technical effects are all big theater."

And Mel Gussow, writing in *The New York Times* of the
performance of Piri Thomas' *The Golden Streets,* said: "At
the premiere whole families were in attendance, even
some wailing babies (which embellished the naturalistic
atmosphere of the play). Unescorted youngsters
crouched on the grass, popping bubble gum, sipping
soda and gluing their eyes to the stage.

"The audience was full of unscreened emotions. They
booed the villain (a junkie), loudly cheered the actress
who chased the villain away from her boy friend, encouraged stage romance ('Hot Dog, don't you have nobody to dance with?'), laughed when things got too melo-
dramatic, applauded the author's well-chosen slang, and
seemed warmed by ethnic references, particularly the humorous ones."

Among other works Miriam Colón and her troupe
have produced for the streets of New York are Maxwell

117

Anderson's *Winterset,* Lorca's *The Evil Spell of the Butterfly,* and Ernesto Fuentes' *The Eagle and the Serpent.* The group in its six-times-a-week performances also one season staged *A Dramatized Anthology of Puerto Rican Short Stories.* From her original funding of a few hundred dollars, Miriam now has a budget which ranges annually from $120,000 to $150,000.

"It is never enough," she said.

The money comes from assorted sources. A partial list includes the National Foundation for the Arts, both the Rockefeller Foundation and the Rockefeller Brothers Fund, the New York Foundation, the Astor Foundation, the Avon Fund, and the Chase Manhattan Bank, plus, of course, state and city support. For the first several years Miriam drew no salary but recently has allocated herself $150 a week. "It pays expenses."

The Puerto Rican National Theater accepts one hundred students each year. Over the theater's short history many nationalities have been represented.

"We get Dominicans, *puertorriqueños,* blacks, whites, mixed. We take them from age fourteen on up and we've graduated almost as many adults as youngsters. Sometimes a mother brings a child, remains to watch and stays on herself, or maybe that process will be reversed. We hold two sessions nightly—5:30 to 7:30 and 7:30 to 9:30—and, of course, on Saturdays. That way we don't interfere with school or jobs."

The theater has a staff. "It is more or less permanent," said Miss Colón. "We have classes from January to May and, of course, can only pay people for that period, so all of them have other jobs in other theater work, including acting." These include José Ocasio, Aníbal Otero, Charlie

Creasup, Allan Davis, Iris Martinez.

"Charlie is the stage manager and Allan handles the administration problems, and there are a lot of them. José Ocasio is an actor who performs, teaches, and directs, as does Iris. Aníbal Otero is a scenic designer. He shuttles back and forth between New York and the island."

The Performing Laboratory Unit has its classes in a loft on 18th Street. Rehearsals and the chorus are held there, too. Miriam keeps all the organization's records on the second floor of her home in an efficient-looking little office complete with rows of filing cabinets and an automatic mailer. The office is just off a large living room with a fireplace. Three of the walls are covered with a mélange of pictures and tapestries. The fourth side is mostly a large window which looks out over the garden.

Any conversation with Miriam at home is subject to interruptions. There are phone calls and people. She disappears from the garden and it is apparent that the chairs around the dining room table are filling up.

Settling down in her chair again with Tiny in her lap (she knows it is Tiny because of an almost undiscernible crook at the tip of his tail), Miriam can herself relax instantly, almost catlike. She looks over the garden, and at the ripening apples. It is a pleasant place. She nods toward the dining room and the group around the table.

"I have become a sort of a clearing house for Latin types on television," she said. "A network will call me and say they need so-and-so type and send over a script. Sometimes they also send along the tryout people; sometimes I get them.

"They come along here and study the scripts. Then I

hear them and make the selections right here. The networks take my judgment.

"There are three there now studying for one part. One is so much better than the others he is almost sure to get it. But even reading for the tryout is good experience."

Do the networks pay her for this service to them?

"No, but they are good to me. I'm happy to do them a favor."

JULIO ROSADO DEL VALLE
Painter

JULIO ROSADO DEL VALLE was born in the town of Cataño, west across the bay from San Juan, where his father was a barber, and Julio's first painting was done with brushes that had been discarded by his father. As a boy he used to go up on the roof of his home and spend hours dreamily contemplating the colors of the other buildings and their roofs—the blacks, whites, ochres, reds, and greens. He mixed his first colors in the shop of a family friend, Facundo Figueroa, who was the local sign painter and quite a talented copyist.

The Rosado del Valle family was poor and there was little money for non-necessities, so Julio made his paints from white shoe liquid mixed with cooking oils and anything else he could conveniently find. The results were sometimes unusual. When he was in the fifth grade he painted a landscape with a cow in the mid-foreground.

"My teacher thought it was a horse."

The hours spent on the roof as a child are reflected in his colors and his work: the wide range of grays with their differing qualities and transparency, their tonal refractions; the way he uses sun and changing light; the color moods of the clouds, growing plants, mists, shadows, and fog.

121

His works often show the simple things of the island, the traces of the sun when it is setting over the hills of the Cordillera, or a *"ropa tendida al sol,"* a line full of clothes hung out to dry. One critic wrote of him: "His work reminds one of the *guanábana* fruit, greenish black and rough on the outside and marvelously white and delicious on the inside."

Julio was born in 1922 and began to paint with some seriousness when he was in high school in Bayamón, a small town near Cataño. He held his first one-man show in the school in 1944. A year later he had an invited exhibition at the Ateneo Puertorriqueño in San Juan, and that year he also started formal training with Cristóbal Ruiz, who was born in Spain but became a well-known Puerto Rican painter.

In 1946 the University of Puerto Rico awarded Julio a scholarship to the New School for Social Research in New York where he studied with the Cuban, Mario Carreño, and the Ecuadorian muralist, Camilo Egas. He was at the school for two years and during this time lived in New York's Greenwich Village. It was a period when the country was emerging from a long war and the young artists of that era, many of them liberated from the military, converged on the Village where they worked and talked and argued endlessly about painting and techniques, and sometimes starved traditionally. Both the abstracts and the impressionists were popular; cubism and surrealism were emerging. It was a heady time and it left a strong impression on Rosado del Valle.

The years of 1947 and 1948 saw him in Europe, first in Italy and then in France. In Florence he studied both the old and more modern masters and experimented with fresco work. He lived in the Pension Merlini, which had formerly been a palace, and covered many of its ancient marble walls with murals which, he found, was a good way to display his work to buyers. And there were some. From Florence he went to Paris and lived in the Rue Cujas on the Left Bank.

The Rue Cujas runs between the Boulevard Saint Michel and the Place Sainte Genevieve, crossing the Rue Saint Jacques on its way there. The Boulevard Saint Germain is just a few blocks away; so are the Sorbonne, the Seine, and Notre Dame. The area abounds in artists and studios and students and sidewalk cafes. Here, too, the war was only recently over. Food was still scarce and decent living places almost impossible. But despite this, a young painter with very little money could find a cheap, if unheated, room and there was always the delicious and durable French bread at controlled prices. And, as Rosado del Valle did, the young painter could happily study and paint and chain-smoke the pestilential French Gauloise Bleus on his way to recognition and maybe even fame.

The black market that had been founded during Hitler's war still flourished and a successful artist might find his work being sought by illicit money operators in search of a solid commodity in exchange for sometimes an embarrassingly large and unaccountable number of francs. Julio did not reach this eminence at this point in life.

The end of the decade saw him back in San Juan where he became a consultant for the División de Educación de la Communidad and the University of Puerto Rico. The director, Irene Delano at that time, was making use of the island's artists by putting them to work on commercial

123

projects while still leaving them time for the traditional. Rosado del Valle illustrated books, designed silk screen prints and posters, worked on films. And at the same time he continued to paint the things he wanted to paint.

He had exhibits at the Riverside Museum in New York. He sent a painting he had done in Paris to a contest in New York where it won honorable mention and was purchased by the Architectural League. He had his paintings shown in Houston and at the Museo de Bellas Artes in Mexico City. He did a mural on one of the walls of the Caribe Hilton in the early 1950s. It was titled *Vejigates* and portrays the evil spirits which populate the folklore of the island. (It is on a wall of the stairs leading to the gaming rooms.) He painted another mural, this one on a wall at the old Isla Grande Airport. After the new airport came into use, the old terminal was turned into a warehouse and recent visitors to the building were unable to find the mural. It had either been covered with crates and barrels or painted over.

The next several years saw a succession of exhibits for Rosado del Valle: in New York, Washington, at the Primera Bienal Interamericana de Mexico, in Madrid where at an exposition of Arte Actual en España y America he showed three oils and three sketches, and at many in Puerto Rico, mostly San Juan and Ponce.

There are, of course, other sides of the artist. His first marriage when he was quite young was brief in duration. He next married the daughter of Governor Luis Muñoz Marín, Muna Muñoz Lee, who bore him two daughters and a son before this marriage, too, ended in divorce. He then married Almah Núñez and they have one child, born in 1974.

JULIO ROSADO DEL VALLE

Professor Ernesto J. Ruiz de la Matta, special assistant for cultural affairs to the Resident Commissioner of Puerto Rico in Washington, has been a close friend of Rosado del Valle since the early 1950s and has done a monograph of the artist, *Apuntes en Torno a la Obra de Julio Rosado del Valle,* scheduled for publication by the Institute of Puerto Rican Culture. Professor Ruiz de la Matta took his bachelor's degree from the University of Puerto Rico in Art History, with special emphasis on seventeenth-century art in Holland and Spain. After a master's at Harvard he tends now to be more interested in Latin-American art.

Ruiz de la Matta believes Rosado del Valle to be by all odds the greatest painter Puerto Rico has produced, and doubtless would think so even if the artist was not a close friend. In this he is joined by Marta Traba, a prominent South American art critic who considers Rosado del Valle to be the artist "through which Puerto Rican painting enters fully into the current modern scene."

"He is also a good friend and companion," said Ruiz de la Matta. "He used to drink heavily, too much, but he went on the wagon in the late 1950s and hasn't touched a drop of liquor since. He loves coffee, though, and he has a big espresso pot. We used to, with another friend or two, sit around a kitchen table and drink eight or ten pots of coffee and talk till three or four o'clock in the morning.

"He is a very articulate man. In his younger days he was outspoken and impulsive. Later he became more introspective and thoughtful and sedate. He is very soft-spoken and never gets angry. A great sense of humor. He's a good talker but he's also a good listener."

Physically, Rosado del Valle is of medium height and stocky build. Hobbies? "No hobbies. He likes to paint. He works in almost a frenzy. But demands perfection. He has a terrific out-put of work but he probably destroys almost as many canvases as he keeps because he isn't satisfied with them." Another friend and admirer wrote: "His mood of creating is accompanied by a great nervousnéss, an inexplicable restlessness that is expressed in an urge to escape from everything and walk, walk and never stop. It is an anguish he can only find surcease from when he gives himself to the work of using his brush and pallette and canvas to create a painting—usually late at night or early dawn."

In 1955, Rosado del Valle became Artist in Residence for the Higher Educational Council of Puerto Rico, the administrative body of the University, a position he still holds. This gives him an annual honorarium in return for which he does a certain number of paintings a year for the university and sometimes murals, usually on some theme of higher education. He also did a series of paintings for the Antigua Glorieta de Arte on the Rio Piedras campus of the University of Puerto Rico. It was named *A Series of Insects* and all of the subjects, including one of an ant and another of a fly's head, were portrayed heroic in size.

In 1957–58 he returned to New York to study and paint under a Guggenheim fellowship. The sixties, according to a chronology in Professor Ruiz de la Matta's *Apuntes en Torno a la Obra,* took the artist and his paintings to exhibits in Boston; St. Augustine, Florida; Mexico City; Venezuela; Connecticut State College; and in a dozen or more shows on his own island, but most important, for a one-man show at the Pan American Union in Washington, D.C., during May and June of 1965. This show was very successful, both from critical appreciation and a financial point of view.

In 1971, Rosado del Valle staged a one-man exhibit at the Galeria del Morro in San Juan under the general subject of "Love." It consisted of a series of erotic subjects.

"It was most unusual for him," said a friend. "The critics thought it was something he had to get out of his system."

Paintings signed by Rosado del Valle are widely scattered throughout the island and the United States proper. The Pan American Union has at least two. Others are held by such diverse collectors as Muñoz Marín, publisher Gardner Cowles of Des Moines, José Ferrer, and Marlene Dietrich.

"Julio does very well with his painting," said Ruiz de la Matta. "He tried selling through galleries, both in Puerto Rico and on the mainland, but he didn't like that. Now he sells from his home—where he also has his studio. And at shows, of course.

"He's not rich, but I doubt if he really wants to be. And . . . do you know any serious artist who is rich?"

CÓNCHA MELÉNDEZ
Writer and Critic

$\mathcal{B}$Y THE YEAR 1974, Cóncha Meléndez had been retired, in the sense that she no longer taught at the University of Puerto Rico in the Department of Spanish
Studies which she had headed for so long. In her private
life Cóncha Meléndez would never really retire, as any
visitor to her home in the Condado section of Puerto Rico
could quickly see. There was still the neat clutter of
papers around the room she worked in, the smell of ink,
the unmistakable aura of activity.

Three years previously, in 1971, Miss Meléndez had
been named Puerto Rican Woman of the Year. That
same year she was honored by the government of Venezuela which bestowed on her the *Condecoration de la Orden
de Andrés Bello* in recognition of her distinguished work in
literature and in appreciation of the gentle but pervasive
influence she had exercised for many years on the writers
of Puerto Rico—from poetry, to essays, to short stories—
and her efforts in making known the literature of Latin
America to the rest of the world.

Cóncha Meléndez' earliest writing was poetry, and it
was first published when she was twelve years old. By the
time she retired her work totalled several volumes of collected poetry, including her own and literary criticism,

and she was widely known throughout the Hispanic world, esteemed almost equally as a writer, critic, and teacher.

Cóncha Meléndez was born on November 23, 1904, in Caguas, a town south of San Juan. Her parents were Francisco Meléndez-Valero and Carmen Ramírez de Meléndez, and when Cóncha was seven years old they moved to Rio Piedras, then a suburb of San Juan where the University was located and now part of the spreading city itself.

By the time Cóncha was twelve she was already reciting her own poetry in public and had had several poems published. Of these, the magazine *Puerto Rico Illustrado* commented that although her work was not, of course, fully developed, it gave an insight into the kind of "strong, forceful writing of which she will be capable."

She was a pretty girl, almost tiny, with curly black hair and steady black eyes, and was a normal, slightly mischievous child. In a recent interview she recalled playing tricks on her younger sister. She also remembered slipping away from home one day with a boy companion to ride on a merry-go-round, horrifying her parents, not because she had slipped away or ridden the carrousel, but because the boy was not related, not even a cousin.

After high school Cóncha enrolled in the University, taking her bachelor's degree in 1922. Two years later she went to Madrid where she did graduate work at the Centro de Estudios Históricos. Returning to the University of Puerto Rico in 1925, she was combining her own studies with teaching when the University decided to establish a Department of Spanish Studies and sent her, and another gifted student, Antonio S. Pedreira, to Columbia University in New York to get master's degrees. They returned in 1927 and Pedreira, who himself was destined to become one of Puerto Rico's best-known writers, became head of the new department and Doña Cóncha became one of the first teachers.

Her career continued to be linked with Pedreira's for many years. When he went to Madrid to get his doctorate in 1931, she went to the National University of Mexico where she became the first woman ever to receive a doctorate in literature from that institution, the oldest establishment of higher learning on the North American continent. Her degree by academic designation was *Doctor en Felosofia y Latros.* Her highly praised dissertation was in the field of Latin-American literature. (Thirty-nine years later, in August of 1970, Cóncha Meléndez again niched out a small footnote to Mexico's history when she returned to its capital city to be the first woman to lecture at the Academia Mexicana de la Lengua. Her subject was the Mexican poet, Amado Nervo, and the occasion the 100th anniversary of his birth.)

In 1932 both she and Pedreira returned to the University of Puerto Rico. At this time the University established the Chair for Hispanic-American Studies, which Miss Meléndez occupied until her retirement in 1967, even after Pedreira's death in 1959, at which time she succeeded him as head of the department.

During these years Doña Cóncha initiated several generations of Puerto Rican students into an affection for Hispanic studies and trained many, many teachers as well. Her classes were always popular. Enrique Laguerre, the well-known Puerto Rican writer, said of her:

"Her classes were inspiring. She went far beyond the

CÓNCHA MELÉNDEZ

text and she had the ability to transmit to the student a
need for betterment, a love for noble ideals and a balanced sense of life." Some of her ability to motivate her
students to those noble ideals may have come from Dr.
Meléndez' own devotion to them. She was always deeply
religious and, after her retirement, she spent a great deal
of her time in helping further the aims of the Escuela
Unity de Cristianismo Práctico, a religious organization.

She was a prolific writer—prose, poetry, and literary
criticism—and is probably most renowned internationally
for the latter. Her first prose book, published by Columbia University, was a study of Amado Nervo, in which she
examined both the writing and the man, his viewpoints,
outlook, humor—and how all of these things affected his
work. Following this, she published her doctoral dissertation under the title, *"The Novela Indianista en Hispano-
america"* ("The Indian Influence of Latin-American Fic-
tion").

She wrote, actually, about almost all the influential au-
thors of Latin America, including Alfonso Reyes of Mexico; Rubén Darío of Nicaragua; Pablo Neruda of Chile;
Andrés Bello of Venezuela; Enrique Laguerre, José de
Diego, Luis Muñoz Rivera, and Luis Palés Matos of
Puerto Rico; José Martí of Cuba; and of her colleague, Antonio Pedreira.

Her collected writings are heterogeneous. The first volume includes many of her lectures, remembrances of her
childhood, and résumés of her work. Her second is a
collection of Hispanic-American poetry, including the
work of Darío, Neruda, Muñoz Rivera, and Palés Matos.

The third is an account of people she has known,
largely literary, her conversations with them, and her

131

book reviews. Volume four is the poetry of Alfonso Reyes, with introduction and comments. Her book, *José de Diego en Mi Memories,* contains ten essays she wrote on this Puerto Rican poet and patriot in which she comments on his personality as it shows through his work. She has published two anthologies of short stories.

The outlook and vision of Cóncha Meléndez were far broader than her native Puerto Rico. Lecture tours and her own personal curiosity to see and understand other cultures took her into virtually all of Latin America and to the United States, including such disparate destinations as Missouri, New York City, Vermont, and Arkansas.

In Arkansas she had been requested to speak on the occasion of "Cervantes Day" and at Middleburg College in Vermont she conducted a seminar on the Puerto Rican short story for twenty-five students, one of whom was Argentinian, two Puerto Rican, and the remainder just plain Anglos.

In retirement, Doña Cóncha continued writing and continued to collect the work of other writers, much as other men and women collect paintings or sculpture. A visitor in the middle 1970s found that she still maintained her "professorial look" and commented on her surroundings: "Her home has the quietness of a library, full of books, diplomas, and certificates which bear evidence of her accomplishments over many years. Through a door are a patio, trees, and a small fountain. The fountain reminds one of the marble of the Alhambra. The honk of an auto or the sound of an occasional airplane engine are the only intrusions into this quiet haven."

There is also a mountain in the distance and it may have inspired one of Cóncha Meléndez' poems which, translated into English, reads:

CÓNCHA MELÉNDEZ

I love my country's lofty mountains!
Here, where all is soft and quiet,
They are untamed.
They are the symbol of a hidden power
That germinates through the ages.

Sometimes the storm burst upon their summits;
Into their virgin bosom the dew shakes its tears;
The sun surrounds them with a thousand halos;
The mist offers them fantastic kisses;
But they lift their foreheads
Unmoved before the mysteries that life contains,
Before men's struggles and petty ambitions,
Which are nothing, if seen across unfathomable
Infinite eternity.

The mountains, nearby, are like a glowing hope;
And from afar, like a maiden's dream,
Floating in the blue distance.

Why do they rise thoughtful and serene?
Because they know many things unknown to us;
And in the nights full of blossoms,
The stars have told them the shining destinies
Of all the islands:
The great old past of the Isles of Greece,
The great new future that awaits the Antilles;

Of the genius of a victorious race,
The great deeds of Latin America,
The hymn of the peoples that are unfurling,
One and many at the same time, the banner of
     Bolivar's dream!
The mountains know it,
The mountains lofty and unmoved!

JUSTINO DÍAZ
Operatic Singer

JUSTINO DÍAZ wears a silver looped cross, the Ankh, suspended from a silver chain around his neck. It is the Egyptian symbol of life, and Díaz touches it occasionally as he talks. His daughter wheels a tricycle around the playground of the tall apartment building in New York's upper west side where Díaz and his family live.

He is wearing jeans and a shirt open at the throat. No beard, no mustache; a pleasant openness and an air of well-being, good health, contentment. Aside from a greeting to a visitor half a block away in a rich basso that has been trained to reach the galleries, Díaz might be just about anybody, from a rising young executive to the man who commands the pumps at the nearest filling station and likes doing it. Except, perhaps, for the self-assurance brought by his success as one of the youngest and brightest stars of the Metropolitan Opera Company, and in opera houses around the world.

It was September and Díaz had just returned from Vienna where he had sung in the State Opera House, a Verdi role, and in a day or so he would be going to London and the Royal Festival Hall, for more Verdi, this time *Attila*. A little later he would visit the Hamburg State Opera House for a new production there of Mozart's *The*

Marriage of Figaro; thence to Spain and back for a tour of the United States, including singing Romeo in Gounod's *Romeo and Juliet* in Miami. Then to the Met in the spring. It would be a busy year.

"You like it?"

"I love it."

"People are not always content with their work and their lives, no matter how successful they may be. If you had the chance to go back and start over, would you try for any other career?"

"Oh, no. I sing. I act. I love doing both. It is my life." The Ankh is not inappropriate for Díaz. Life is important to him; he is a very much alive young man.

A moment earlier he had talked of being totally immersed in his work, his singing. And at that moment elder daughter Natasha, born in 1970, left her tricycle for the monkey jungle and climbed to the top. She called to her father with just a touch of regal imperialism befitting a girl whose parents are both stars, Daddy in opera and Mama in ballet.

"Look, Daddy."

"Yes, my love." Not totally immersed.

Justino himself was six when he made his first public appearance at the Robinson grammar school in San Juan. He sang a solo at a music show the school was presenting.

"It was 'Old Black Joe,' " he said. "In English. I can't imagine why."

He was born on January 29, 1940, in the Condado section of San Juan, the only child of Justino Díaz Morales and Gladys Villarini. His father, an economist, taught at the University of Puerto Rico. In 1945 the senior Díaz took his little family to Philadelphia for a year while he was getting his master's degree and in 1954 they all went to Cambridge for a year and a half while he completed the work for a doctorate at Harvard.

After his debut with "Old Black Joe," Justino continued singing. The school had a music teacher and she evidently recognized a quality of the young voice which prompted her to begin his training and to encourage him to sing at every opportunity—in the school chorus and the church choir. Her enthusiasm infected Justino and remained. In Cambridge he attended high school, improving his English (which is almost accentless), and sang in the coed glee club.

Justino returned to San Juan in 1955 with his parents and graduated from high school in 1958. And life was not all school and singing. Like most young *puertorriqueños*, he was an avid baseball fan and played the game with the other boys. His father was a good tennis player and taught Justino, who also became quite expert. There was the ocean, too, of course; virtually everyone in Puerto Rico swims or at least goes to the beach.

He sang in his first opera while still in high school. San Juan had an annual "opera season" and the company, which usually had eight or ten guest stars, always needed "supers." When a friend proposed that the two of them volunteer to be "spear carriers," Justino went along happily and from that vantage point his father had enough influence to help get him into the chorus. He remembers very well his first performance in *La forza del destino* by Giuseppe Verdi, and the second in *Lucia di Lammermoor* by Gaetano Donizetti. Both were in Italian, of course. "I learned the words by rote."

From this original entry into the operatic field Justino

progressed in just one year to become a member of the permanent chorus and the next year performed his first solo.

"It was just one line in *Traviata* announcing that dinner was served, but it was very exciting. I was barely eighteen years old. Oh yes, I remember it very well. I can remember 'Old Black Joe,' too.'"

Justino enrolled at the University of Puerto Rico where he both studied and sang with María Esther Robles, a soprano of considerable talent and fame. Augusto Rodríguez was director of the University chorus at this time, and for many years afterward. Both Rodríguez and Robles found the young singer a pliant and promising student.

Then, in 1959, Justino went to the New England Conservatory of Music in Boston where he remained for two and a half years studying, among other things, Italian, French, and German. He sang in churches, festivals, anywhere to make a little money.

"I sang 'The Star-Spangled Banner' at a fund-raiser for Nixon," he said, grinning. "Got fifty bucks for it."

He also, while at the Conservatory, sang with the New England Opera Company under the direction of Boris Goldovsky and remembers particularly doing three roles in Rossini's *The Barber of Seville*—Basilio, the singing teacher; Ambrosio, a servant; and a sergeant of the guard. He also received voice lessons from Frederick Jagel, who had formerly been with the Metropolitan Opera Company in New York.

The almost meteoric rise Díaz made into the higher strata of stardom in opera really began in 1962 when he arrived at the Met studios with a letter from Goldovsky, had an audition and was promptly accepted for training. Early in 1963 he entered a contest and won first prize from the Leiderkranz Foundation and then a few weeks later, in March, 1963, he competed in a contest for singers in the United States and Canada. It was held at the Met and Díaz again won first prize—a $2,000 cash scholarship award and—*mas importánte*—a contract to sing at the Met.

He made his debut that same year with the famous opera company, singing the role of Count Monterone in Verdi's *Rigoletto*. It was the same opera and the same stage where Enrico Caruso had made his Met debut in 1903, just sixty years earlier. Caruso had been thirty at the time. Díaz was just twenty-three.

For the next three years he had roles in and out of the Met: the Inquisitor in *Don Carlos* and the High Priest in *Aïda*, both by Verdi; Don Basilio, Figaro, and Don Giovanni in the Mozart operas; Mephistopheles in Gounod's *Faust*. He also sang in oratorios, recitals, and music festivals, including the Casals Festival in San Juan, the Festival of Two Worlds in Spoleto, Italy, at Salzburg in Austria, and Tanglewood in Massachusetts.

In 1966 he sang at the opening of Lincoln Center in New York City and he admits it was one of the high points of his career. And then went on to others. There was a debut at La Scala in Milan, probably the best-known opera house in the world, in Rossini's *The Siege of Corinth*.

He sang Manrico in *Il Trovatore* at Teatro Colón in Buenos Aires and confirmed there that in 1908 Antonio Paoli, the Puerto Rican tenor who had been known as the "Lion of Ponce," had also made his Argentine debut singing the same role in the same theater.

The Argentine composer Alberto Ginastera so admired the Díaz voice and delivery in this and other performances that he wrote *Beatrix Cenci* and the part of Count Cenci just for him. Díaz sang it at the opening week of the Kennedy Center in Washington, D.C., in 1971 and then later that same year at the Lincoln Center in New York.

From the bench on the playground, Díaz talks easily of his life and his work while he keeps an eye on Natasha, who doesn't much appreciate having her playtime with her much-too-absent father being usurped.

"People who meet me are always surprised," he said, "when I tell them I am an opera singer. 'A Puerto Rican?' they say. They do not think we do cultural things on our little island. They should realize that although we have a very small island we are very large in spirit. And have a great background in our history. One of the reasons I can interpret so many roles is that I am an amalgamation of many civilizations."

He talks then about his wife, Anna Aragno, who is now dancing again after taking time out to have Natasha and Katya, the second daughter, born in 1972. Anna Aragno had formerly been with both the Bolshoi Theater and the Metropolitan Opera Company, where she danced with, among others, Rudolf Nureyev and Edward Villella. Anna and Justino "met at the Met," and were married a year later, in 1966.

Mrs. Díaz is Italian but was living with her parents in London when she came to the United States on a Fulbright exchange fellowship to study and was given permission to dance at the Met. She has been with no other company permanently since, but has danced in Florence, Spoleto, Monte Carlo, and New York. Choreographer Loris Gay created a special dance, "Ophelia," for her, based on the mad scene from Hamlet. Now husband and wife have separate careers which take them apart a great deal, although they try to arrange it so that at least one of them is at home with the children and that they have time for each other.

Natasha wheels by to point out a flaw in the mechanical performance of her cycle. It is the third time and for the third time her father patiently examines and performs the necessary repairs. She is wearing a little shirt her father brought her from London and that is duly admired. Justino tells Natasha he is busy at the moment and admonishes her not to bother Daddy. Set to music it might be a scene from Verdi, if Verdi had ever included a child soprano. And also, Díaz might as well have been talking to a charming, and lovely, pixie.

The two senior Díaz members respect and admire each other's careers. Justino prefers watching ballet to watching opera and Anna has learned to like opera, which she had not originally. They help each other at times.

"Anna has had a great deal more actual stage training than I have," he said. "She has taught me how to move easily and not stiffly. And I can watch a rehearsal and tell her when she is not breathing properly and that is almost as important in ballet as it is in singing."

Do they find that being apart so much creates a problem for their marriage?

"Yes, but it can be solved. We each have two careers, one on the stage and the other at home. We have to work hard at both. And, just as we book our time for opera or ballet, we also have to book it for each other and the children."

Most of the personal opinions Díaz has formed during his thirty-odd years are rather predictable. He prefers women to be feminine. His wife is; Natasha definitely is. When he has time to read he likes biographies. His favorite operas are Mozart and Verdi. In paintings he prefers the impressionists, and he admires *Don Quixote* most among novels he has read.

He also has a concept of the perfect life on earth—eliminate selfishness, hunger, and poverty. And the greatest love is the love of family.

"You grew up in Puerto Rico. You have lived in several parts of the mainland United States and have traveled all over the world. Now you live in New York. Is this a preference or a necessity?"

Díaz laughed. "When one sings principally at the Met and at the Lincoln Center (which is only a few blocks away), living in New York is at least convenient and probably necessary.

"And someone once paid me a compliment. At least I have always taken it as a compliment. He said that I belonged among the *rascacielos.*"

"*Rascacielos?*"

"That's Spanish for skyscrapers."

JAIME BENÍTEZ
Educator

$\mathcal{T}$HE BUZZER ON HIS desk sounded and Jaime Benítez leaped at the phone like it might get away. He answered "Yes" and then listened for a moment. "We want 3 per cent for Puerto Rico," he said. "Tell 'em we don't want any part of less than that."

He returned to his place on the black leather divan in his not-too-big office in the old Longworth Building on Capitol Hill.

"That won't mean anything to Puerto Rico this year," he explained almost in an aside, "but in the two years following it will give us $62 million in federal funds for education. We get $32 million now." And he added: "The money will have to come out of funds which would otherwise be spent on the mainland. The Senate is a little uncertain about it."

Jaime Benítez is the Resident Commissioner of Puerto Rico and as such is its representative in the Congress of the United States. He cannot vote for or against measures on the House floor, although he can, and frequently does, speak there. He can introduce bills and he has a vote on the House Committee on Education and Labor to which he was appointed and on which he serves. He is, also, the only member of the House who serves a term of four years, that being his term as Commissioner.

Benítez is on the small side in stature, a rushing, restless man. His hair is iron grey and he doesn't look his sixty-odd years. His office has the flags of both Puerto Rico and the United States on standards. On a table in one corner stands a sailing ship lovingly designed from sea shells, obviously a gift from a constituent. The walls are colorful with travel posters of his island.

In his first term as Resident Commissioner, Don Jaime was well at home in Washington. He went to college there and visited frequently. As one of the world's foremost educators he has many influential and well-placed friends on the mainland and, unlike an earlier Commissioner, Luis Muñoz Rivera, he does not feel alone nor live "in a tomb-like isolation."

Jaime Benítez was born on October 29, 1908, on the tiny island of Vieques some fifteen or twenty miles off the shores of Puerto Rico. His family were sugar cane planters.

"I came from a wealthy family," he says, grinning, "but unfortunately they were broke by the time I happened along."

Jaime was the eighth son and his childhood was marked by more than ordinary tragedy. "My mother died when I was six, my father when I was seven, and my oldest brother when I was eight."

At that time, after the death of his parents and the brother who had taken care of the younger Benítez brood thereafter, the family moved to San Juan and into the home of a sister, Clotilde. Clotilde was a teacher who sold real estate successfully on the side and it was she who now raised the younger children.

Young Jaime grew up like most middle-class Puerto Rican youngsters of the time. His grades in school were at or near the top but he was an outgoing youngster with plenty of time for playmates. They played boys' games, teased their sisters, and splashed on the beach in the never-ending warmth of a benevolent climate.

In 1926, Clotilde sent Jaime to Georgetown University in Washington to get a law degree. He worked his way through much of the time.

"I was a pretty good soda jerk and I worked in the Census Bureau. I could type. I was sort of a junior clerk."

He received his Bachelor of Law from Georgetown in 1930 and his Master of Law in 1931, graduating second highest in his class and earning a place on the prestigious *Law Journal*. He worked as a library assistant until he passed the District of Columbia bar examination.

"About that time," said Benítez, "the Chancellor of the University of Puerto Rico came to town. He was looking for a substitute instructor to teach political theory and contemporary civilization. I took the job for one year. I stayed forty-one."

The Commissioner looked around the room for a moment, and it was one of the few intervals during a thirty-minute time span that the phone didn't ring nor did anyone knock. "Yes. I stayed forty-one years. And then they kicked me out."

That was on October 8, 1971, and during those forty-one years Benítez had gone from instructor to professor, to Chancellor to President of the University, which had increased its enrollment during the years from three thousand to forty-five thousand students.

"My departure was an overnight thing. One day I was

there. The next day I was out." It was also a political thing, and now "past history."

It had been the time of the Great Depression when the Chancellor came to Georgetown looking for a short-time instructor and looking specifically for Jaime Benítez who had been recommended to him as a bright young man with the necessary credentials, and in those depression days any job was a sanctuary to dive into.

"I took it," says Benítez, "but I had a very hard time of it. During the years in Washington I had forgotten my Spanish. I could teach in English, but now I had to go out and recapture my native language.

"I also found that teaching is not such a cinch. I had to spend about seven hours of work preparing for every class. It was good for me, of course. It was a re-education. I discovered advantages of learning in a way I never could have in any other.

"And during the course of that re-education I also discovered that teaching, for me, was the most meaningful thing I could possibly do."

He served as instructor and professor of Social and Political Science from 1931 to 1942 and during these years found time to collect a Master of Arts degree from the University of Chicago in 1937. He also took time out to get married to the former Luz A. Martínez on August 15, 1941. They have three children, Clotilde, Jaime, and Margarita Inés.

Then in 1942 he was named Chancellor of the University, a position he held until 1966 when he became President, the youngest in the school's history.

"Did this put you in the position so many college and university presidents find themselves—being chiefly a front figure and a fund-raiser?"

"Never. My job was to be an academic leader always, an intellectual leader, to constantly raise the standards of the institution, to open a widening road to education for students of all kinds, from any place or any class.

"I tried to create a center of learning which would attract the best scholars anywhere to the University. And they were to impart to the young men and women in their classes the very best in contemporary education."

He must have succeeded to a more than ordinary degree. Esther Seijo de Zayas is a professor at the University and a member of its Academic Senate. Of her former boss she said: "Don Jaime is an amazing teacher and an amazing writer. He could—and did—inspire other teachers. If you wanted to stay on the staff you had better keep up with him, and if you brought him a question you had better know the subject background. He was amazingly well informed on so many things. He also had firm convictions and he was very frank."

After he was "fired" as President of the University, Benítez could have, had he been willing to swallow his pride, remained at the institution in a professorial capacity. Or he could have practiced law, for he had taken the Puerto Rican bar exams some years back. Those exams entail both written and oral tests and, after passing the written, Benítez invited his students to come and listen when he appeared before the oral board.

"I examine you," he told them. "It is only fair that you should see me examined." Many did, and watched him pass successfully. But, after leaving the University as President, he said: "I didn't want to practice law and I wasn't ready to return to a professorship, or at least not

146

at my own University. So I took a sabbatical."

Which is like taking a walk to collect your thoughts. And the walk brought him very quickly to the decision to enter politics. While he had never taken a serious part in the political activities of the island, he certainly was no stranger to public life. He had presided over the meetings of the Committee on the Bill of Rights of the Constitutional Convention of Puerto Rico in 1951–52. He was a United States delegate to the University Convention in Utrecht in 1948. He served as a member of the American National Commission for UNESCO from 1948 to 1954 and was a delegate to meetings in Paris and Havana. And, in 1957–58, he was President of the National Association of State Universities, a signal honor which marked both his stature as an educator and that of the school as an institution.

Benítez was and had been for years a member of Partido Popular Democrático which had been formed in 1937 by his old and good friend, the former governor, Luis Muñoz Marín. And he had been identified for many years as being an outspoken intellectual figure among the more prominent members of the Popular Democrats.

"Also," said Benítez, "my name was a well-known household word in Puerto Rico. Remember, I had been Chancellor and President for almost twenty years and during that time I had given out about 75,000 diplomas. Most of the men and women who held these diplomas still lived and voted on the island."

Benítez had established his own scholarship by publishing a dozen or so volumes on legal and social sciences, philosophical theory, university education and its problems, and culture and politics in Puerto Rico. He had

147

built the University of Puerto Rico into an intellectual institution well known throughout the United States and the world. And he had scores of friends in Washington where he was a familiar figure both in educational areas and in the Congress where he had often appeared to testify on federal aid to education.

So it was not surprising that in 1972 he ran for and was elected to the office of Resident Commissioner, one of the two major elective offices on the island. The governor, of course, is the other.

As a member of the House Education and Labor Committee, the same committee on which his fellow Puerto Rican, Herman Badillo of New York, has a seat, Commissioner Benítez (or Congressman; the terms are used interchangeably) is able to carry forward his chief interests: education, of course, but also the welfare, labor conditions, wage situations, and social conditions of his island.

There are three political factions on the island, or at least three major ones: those who believe that Puerto Rico is best off under the present Commonwealth situation; those who would rather see the island and its roughly three million people as a separate state; and those who want complete independence.

Benítez is strongly in favor of the Commonwealth status, believing that it gives the Puerto Rican people many advantages over statehood, some of them being, as he says:

• The basic social, civic, economic, and educational rights of American citizenship as they are backed up by federal resources, federal legislation, and federal courts.

• The rights and duties of common defense with the

stability and the solidarities inherent in such common responsibility.

• The free access of Puerto Ricans to mainland job opportunities and the free access of Puerto Rican goods to mainland marketing opportunities.

• The exclusion of Puerto Rico from direct federal taxation, thereby creating a federal tax-free zone which facilitates necessary industrial development in Puerto Rico.

• The provision that all taxes collected under the internal revenue laws of the United States, on articles produced in Puerto Rico and transported to the United States, or consumed in the island, shall be converted into the treasury of Puerto Rico.

"Under statehood," says Congressman Benítez, "some of these would be lost. Under independence, all would be lost."

The rivalry between the Popular Democrats, who stand for the Commonwealth status for Puerto Rico, and the New Progressive Party, which favors statehood, has always been strong but it also has been marked by moderation and a reasonable amity. This has also been true of the Independence Party. However, the Nationalist Party has had a path noted for violence since its inception. Its activities reached a high point in terrorism during the early 1950s under the leadership of Pedro Albizu Campos, leader of the Nationalist Party of that day, and a passionate advocate of independence. Out of many violent incidents, two reached directly and deeply into the government of the United States.

The first, on November 1, 1950, was an attempt to assassinate President Harry Truman and resulted in a gun battle in front of Blair House on Pennsylvania Avenue, a battle witnessed by hundreds of people in the streets. One Puerto Rican and one White House guard were killed; one Puerto Rican and two guards were wounded.

It happened a little after two o'clock in the afternoon. Griselio Torresola, thirty, a *puertorriqueño* resident of New York, was on the north side of the street, a little west of Blair House, which was being used as a temporary Presidential residence while the White House was being renovated. Blair House is diagonally across the street from the White House.

Oscar Collazo, thirty-six, the second Puerto Rican, also of New York City, was across a side street and to the east. In front of Blair House were Secret Service agent Floyd Boring, and White House guard Joseph O. Davidson, standing by a small, wooden guard booth. Stationed in front of Lee House, next door, were guards Leslie Coffelt and Joseph Downs. Standing on the Blair House steps was guard Donald T. Birdzell.

Collazo walked by Boring and Davidson until he reached the sidewalk in front of the Blair House steps. There he pulled a German Walther P-38 from his pocket and started firing at Birdzell whose back was momentarily turned.

In order to draw fire away from the President's temporary home (Mr. Truman was upstairs taking a nap, clad in his underwear; his wife and his wife's mother were in another part of the house), Birdzell ran into Pennsylvania Avenue.

Collazo followed Birdzell with the pistol fire and as Birdzell turned to return the fire he was hit. He dropped to one knee and continued firing. Davidson and Boring, who were standing by the guard booth also drew weapons and began firing at Collazo. He fell wounded.

As this crossfire started, Torresola came from the west and approached Coffelt and Downs who were standing by another guard booth in front of Lee House. When he was only a few feet away he pulled a German Luger and began shooting. Both men returned the fire but both were hit as Torresola emptied the entire clip of the Luger. Torresola himself was killed instantly with a bullet in the head from their return fire. Coffelt died of his wounds.

A letter written in Spanish was found in Torresola's clothing, signed by Albizu Campos. It delegated authority to "my dear Griselio" to "assume the leadership of the [Nationalist] movement in the U.S. if necessary." Collazo was tried, convicted, and sentenced to death. President Truman commuted the sentence to life imprisonment. That was incident number one.

Then on March 4, 1954, three Puerto Rican men and one woman stationed in the visitors' gallery sprayed the floor of the House of Representatives with bullets, some twenty to twenty-five, fired from two German Lugers and two Walther P-38s. Five Congressmen were wounded: Rep. Alvin M. Bentley, thirty-five, of Michigan; Rep. Ben F. Jensen, sixty-one, of Iowa; Rep. Clifford Davis, fifty-six, of Tennessee; Rep. George Fallon, fifty-one, of Maryland; and Rep. Kenneth A. Roberts, forty-one, of Alabama.

Arrested in the gallery with the weapons were Lolita Lebrón, thirty-four, of New York; Rafael Cancel Miranda, twenty-five, of Brooklyn; and Andrés Figuero

Cordero, twenty-nine, of New York. Shortly thereafter Irving Flores Rodríguez, twenty-seven, also of New York, implicated by Mrs. Lebrón, was arrested at Union Station in Washington. All were Puerto Ricans.

Mrs. Lebrón, who claimed she was the leader of the plot, said the assassins had bought one-way tickets from New York, expecting to die in the attack. She was later linked with the same Nationalists who had tried to kill Mr. Truman.

All four were tried and convicted in Washington and on July 9, 1954, Lolita Lebrón was sentenced to serve for 16 years, 8 months in prison; her companions from 25 to 75 years each.

Benítez has little sympathy for the independence cause because of its economic blindness; Puerto Rico is not now and has little chance soon of being self-supporting in the very basic matter of balancing export and import trade, of providing jobs which will produce enough to pay the cost of feeding, housing, and clothing its populace. And he has no sympathy whatsoever with the violence which at times became the hallmark of the Nationalist cause.

He knows, however, as do most of the other moderate leaders of the island, that many Puerto Ricans consider the men and women who espouse and carry out assassination attempts to be superpatriots who are fighting for the freedom of the Puerto Rican people. Those who die, those who go to prison will, if they haven't already, become part of the folklore of the island. Freedom is a bright and shining word. It can mean different things to different people; something as simple, perhaps, as freedom from swinging the machete against the stalk of the sugar cane. And who is to say that Griselio Torresola was not a martyr to a cause that he believed in?

Conceding this, Benítez points out that in 1972, with 85 per cent of the people voting, including eighteen-year-olds for the first time, 60 per cent voted for Commonwealth status, 35 per cent for statehood, and only 5 per cent for independence.

"The Commonwealth status for Puerto Rico is not perfect and those of us who represent it are well aware of that. If it is not perfect, neither is it static. It is a continuing process. It provides the people of Puerto Rico with a flexible political structure within which their spiritual, social, economic, and personal life may continue to advance in civilized, livable, worthwhile, meaningful ways."

In passing, he will mention that present-day Puerto Rican standards of living rank a strong third in this hemisphere, close behind the standards of the United States and Canada. And he adds: "There is only one forum authorized to change the government of Puerto Rico. The forum is not the United Nations, nor the Organization of American States, nor even the United States itself. That forum which has heretofore expressed its full endorsement of the principles of Commonwealth, and which will have to agree to any change before it can be done, is constituted by the people of Puerto Rico."

LA FAMILIA FIGUEROA
Musicians

THE FIGUEROA dynasty of music in Puerto Rico began in the earliest years of the twentieth century with the union of Jesús Figueroa and Carmen Sanabria. Today their decendants, all apparently endowed at birth with the ability to master the violin, the cello, the viola, and the piano, make up probably the most musically accomplished family in the world.

Its most famous member is José ("Pepito") Figueroa, violinist, who has been honored world-wide as a soloist, concert master, and leading member of the internationally-known Figueroa Quintet, composed of José and four brothers.

Jesús Figueroa, founder of the dynasty, was born in Aguadilla in 1878 and grew up to a widely varied musical career. He played the clarinet in the town's Volunteer Band during his early years and then went off, for reasons no one is quite sure of today, to Santo Domingo where he became a member of the Orazama Battalion Band. He next returned to Puerto Rico, to San Juan, to play in the Insular Police Band, thence out to the suburb of Rio Piedras where he was director of the Municipal Band and of a *zarzuela*—a group which presents operettas. And then back again to San Juan where he directed, in turn, the orchestras of the Cine Luna and the Rialto.

Later years saw him directing the San Juan Municipal Band and playing in the symphony. He composed musical pieces in many forms—waltzes, concertos, *danzas*. And he frequently was guest conductor for various musical groups.

Carmen Sanabria de Figueroa was born on January 9, 1882, also in Aguadilla. She started her study of the piano early and in her late teens, when her teacher, Francisca Castañer, returned to her native Spain, she left her most talented pupil in charge of the other students. The Sanabria family was poor and much of the burden of support for several younger brothers fell on Carmen, requiring her to pass up a scholarship to study in Spain in order that she might continue teaching. She did, however, study in San Juan under the accomplished Henry Ern who also taught two of her sons, Pepito and Kachiro.

Carmen and Jesús were married in 1903 and, of course, spent most of their later lives in San Juan. They had, all told, eleven children, of whom eight were living in 1937. Doña Carmen was accompanist for almost all of the famous artists who visited Puerto Rico during her years there and, with the aid of her daughters Carmelina, Angelina, and Leonor, she founded and ran two academies of music in San Juan.

Carmen Figueroa died in 1954 and Jesús Figueroa in 1971. The eight children, all musicians, were José, violin; Narciso, piano; Leonor, piano; Jaime (who has always been known as Kachiro), violin; Carmelina, piano; Angelina, piano; Guillermo, viola; and Rafael, cello.

There is also a third generation, the more musically accomplished among them being the children of Kachiro—Narciso and Rafael, who play the violin and cello respectively—and the offspring of Guillermo—Guillermito and Yvonne, who play the violin and the piano.

José ("Pepito") Figueroa was born on March 25, 1905. In 1911, when he was six years old, his parents gave him a toy violin on Three Kings Day and the boy was fascinated with his Christmas present. More or less formal lessons followed and in 1914 he began serious study with Henry Ern.

When he was still in his early teens, José was booked on concert tours of Mexico and Cuba, both excursions intended for raising money for study in Europe. This dream was realized when, on July 8, 1923, he left for Madrid to study at the Real Conservatorio de Música y Declamación in Madrid. Two years later, on June 27, 1925, he won the *Premio Sarasate,* playing Beethoven's Concerto in A. The prize was four thousand *pesetas* and a splendid-looking diploma from the Conservatorio.

He made a triumphant return to the island the following year, performing Beethoven concerts in several parts of the island and helping in a signal family honor by playing at the San Juan Municipal Theater accompanied by an orchestra which his father was conducting.

Early 1927 saw José in Paris at the Ecole Normale de Musique where he graduated on July 11, 1928, with his degree and high honors. The Paris Symphony Orchestra offered him a place but he refused because he would have had to become a French citizen and this he did not want to do. In 1929 he did accept a post as professor at the Ecole, remaining there for something over a year.

He was invited at this time to play a concert at Roerich

156

Hall in New York and did, although the trip was saddened by the death of his old friend and teacher, Henry Ern, who bequeathed Figueroa his Stradivarius and music library.

For his concert at the Roerich, the *Herald Tribune* critic had high praise, which was echoed a little later when *Le Monde Musical* called him "one of the most complete violinists of his time."

In the meantime two other members of the Figueroa family were coming along musically. Both had left the island in the mid-1920s to study in Madrid, Narciso the piano and Kachiro the violin. Narciso was four years older and kept an eye on the younger Kachiro, but neither worried as much as José. He was more or less responsible for a fair share of their support in Madrid and money was not too plentiful. Any time he gave a concert he would rush out afterwards, fee in hand, to the nearest cable office to send money off to his brothers. "He didn't even wait to read the reviews," a friend said.

Kachiro started studying at the age of sixteen at the Royal Conservatory in Madrid and graduated at eighteen, winning first prize in both violin and chamber music.

Later he recalled the competition. "I started out calm and cool," he said, "but then I got more and more nervous as the piece went on. By the time I was through I was ready to collapse."

The jury of five was unanimous in its decision.

"We went to a restaurant afterwards and I was so overcome I couldn't eat. It was all right though. My brother ate enough for both of us. Narciso was nervous but it had just made him hungry."

By 1930 all five brothers were in Paris. José was professor of violin at the Ecole Normale and first violinist in the Ecole Quartet and also *concertino* (soloist) in the chamber orchestra directed by the famous Alfred Cortot. Guillermo and Rafael were studying at the Ecole Normale. Narciso and Kachiro had completed their studies and were busy playing with groups as well as giving concerts of their own. And at times they teamed up with José, notably at the International Henri Wieniawski Competition in Warsaw where they, in the words of a critic, "added to the laurels of the family."

Then, about 1932, youngest son Rafael graduated as a cellist and the brothers Figueroa gave their first concert as a quintet. It was in Paris under the direction of Cortot, and so successful that the director suggested the group should be formalized and the brothers agreed. Although they at times still played individually, most of their performances for the next several years were as a fivesome and they became famous in the musical world of Europe.

At the outbreak of World War II, in 1939, the brothers returned to Puerto Rico where they dominated the serious music life of the island for the next quarter of a century, and more. Meanwhile their mother and sisters founded the Escuelas Libres de Música, and later the Escuela Figueroa, also in San Juan.

José and Narciso gave a concert in Washington in 1942. The brothers played as a quintet in Carnegie Hall in 1948, and they gave other five-man concerts over the years, both in the United States mainland and in South America. Critic Alton Adams, writing of the family in the *Puerto Rico World Journal* in 1944, said:

"It has been said that the true greatness of a country or

158

nation is judged largely by the leaders it has contributed toward the progress and well-being of humanity in its various fields of activity. If . . . this is a true evaluation the people of Puerto Rico should justly feel spiritually rich and may rightfully claim an enviable position of eminence in the recreative art of music by virtue of its unique and distinguished Figueroa family.

"Like Johann Sebastian Bach of Eisenach and his distinguished sons, Jesús Figueroa and his wife (both musicians of note) have given to the musical world in general and to Puerto Rico, their island home, in particular, sons and daughters the equal of any family . . . that may be found in the annals of recreative musical art."

A picture of the family, published by *Puerto Rico Ilustrado* in 1945, shows them grouped in musical formation, in what one suspects might not have been a too unusual Sunday afternoon family gathering. Leonor and Narciso are at the two pianos. José and Kachiro are with violins, and Guillermo the viola. Don Jesús is playing the bass. Carmelina and Angelina stand by the pianos to turn the pages of the sheet music. Mama is listening.

At the close of 1974 all of the eight children were living and active except Leonor, who died in July of 1955. All of the boys married and the children of Kachiro and Guillermo produced four members of a musical third generation. The other grandchildren found other occupations. José's son, also José but known as Pepe, was attending American University in Washington, D.C., in 1974, and another boy, Jordán, was still in high school.

The two sons of Kachiro are Narciso and Rafael, named for their uncles; Narciso plays the violin and Rafael the cello. The children of Guillermo are Yvonne, born February 11, 1951, and Guillermito, born on April 5, 1953. Guillermito plays the violin and Yvonne the piano.

Guillermo, Jr., started his studies quite naturally with his father, and at thirteen entered the Conservatory of Music in Puerto Rico, where he studied with his distinguished uncle, José Figueroa, for four years. He won scholarships to attend the Musical Camp at Interlochen, Michigan, where he was concert master and soloist of the World Youth Symphony. He was also the youngest soloist and member of the Puerto Rican Symphony Orchestra. At seventeen he entered the Julliard School and during the Christmas season of 1971–72 was concertmaster and soloist of the New York String Orchestra at Carnegie Hall. He was, in 1974, principal violinist of the Julliard Theater Orchestra.

Yvonne Figueroa graduated from high school in Puerto Rico and immediately enrolled in the Conservatory where she also studied with another talented and famous uncle, Narciso, the *pianista*. In 1968, at the age of seventeen, she was awarded the Pablo Casals scholarship for study at the Marlboro Music Festival in Vermont, and the following year went to the National Music Camp at Interlochen, making her appearance there a year ahead of her younger brother. She followed family tradition by graduating *magna cum laude* from both the Escuelas Libres de Música, headed by her aunt Carmelina, and from the Conservatory in Puerto Rico where at least two of her famous uncles could be found instructing at all times.

Guillermito had made his debut at the age of nine in an appearance at the Tapia Theater in San Juan after he had already won a violin competition in New York. By 1964 he and sister Yvonne were giving duet concerts. In 1969 the brother-sister team was broken up when Yvonne married concert violinist Yosef Yankelev and the two began giving performances together. Yvonne also gave a recital at Carnegie Hall and appeared on National Educational Television.

In 1974, the Yankelevs toured Europe in concert, making a dozen or more appearances. They then returned to Puerto Rico to work on their Musica para el Pueblo, Inc., a sister organization of Music for People, Inc., in New York. It seeks to bring concerts directly to the communities, usually in a series of three or four, most of them geared to young people. Yvonne is the founder and executive director of the organization and her husband is musical director.

During the European tour Yvonne took part in the Robert Schumann Festival in East Berlin, in November, and was awarded fifth prize. This was the first time since the creation of the German Democratic Republic that artists from non-Communist countries had been permitted to participate in such an event. Yvonne thus became the first westerner to win an artistic prize in East Germany.

And, in the meantime, the older generation was still going strong. The quintet under the leadership of Don José made triumphant tours of Latin America in the years 1959 and again in 1969, the later of which included an appearance at the presidential palace in San Salvador.

Then, in 1973, they made a tour *nostálgico* of their old stamping grounds in Europe, playing in Paris, Lisbon, Barcelona, Vienna, Salzburg, Graz, and London. In Paris they found many of their former colleagues. They received rave notices from the critics who marveled both at the quintet's matured and well-trained excellence, and at its joint and collective durability. They had to refuse dozens of invitations to perform and were lionized socially in every city.

In New York, where she was preparing for her European tour in 1974, Yvonne Figueroa Yankelev commented on her famous family. "We all seem to have the same temperament," she said. "There is very little of the tempestuous. My grandfather, Don Jesús, was a very calm man. And Don José, who is now head of the family since my grandfather died, is very cool.

"He is not a tall man," she said, "but he has a presence which makes itself felt. He leads the quintet, of course; it is hard to imagine him in any musical group he didn't lead. He is so famous and so respected."

Yvonne herself is something of a beauty with a striking figure, long dark hair and deeply dark eyes; at the piano she is thoughtful, contemplative, but there is never any doubt that she also is in total command of her performance.

Like the other Figueroas, she stays cool. It does run in the family.

INDEX

INDEX